Fighting the Unbeatable Foe

Cover art, interior illustrations, and maps by Ewan Tallentire.
Cover design by D.J. Natelson.

Grateful acknowledgement is given to the following publishers and copyright owners for permission to reprint brief quotes from their publications:

Oral History of William Hudson, World War II Marine, interviewed by Paul Stillwell, Copyright © 2005 by the Pritzker Military Museum and Library.

Brief quotes from pp. 164, 168, 186, 258, 288 [one standalone, one used as an epigraph] from DUTY: A FATHER, HIS SON AND THE MAN WHO WON THE WAR BY BOB GREENE. Copyright ©2000 by Bob Greene. Reprinted by permission of HarperCollins Publishers.

Brief quotes from *Atoms in the Family* by Laura Fermi, published by University of Chicago Press, © 1954 by The University of Chicago.

Quotations from the book THE LIONS OF IWO JIMA by Fred Haynes and James A. Warren. Copyright © 2008 by Major General Fred Haynes (USMC-ret) and James A. Warren. Used by permission of Henry Holt and Company, LLC. All rights reserved.

Outskirts Press, Inc.
http://www.outskirtspress.com

ISBN: 978-1-4787-4206-7

Library of Congress Control Number: 2014959550

Outskirts Press and the "OP" logo are trademarks belonging to Outskirts Press, Inc.

PRINTED IN THE UNITED STATES OF AMERICA

FIGHTING THE UNBEATABLE FOE
Iwo Jima and Los Alamos

Karen Jo Tallentire

Outskirts Press, Inc.
Denver, Colorado

Table of Contents

Introduction

When an unstoppable force meets an immovable object, who wins?
Which side was the truly unbeatable foe?

Even if you do not choose war, war can come to you. Sometimes your only choice is to win the war or be killed. Sometimes your enemy refuses to surrender. Are you willing to kill every single enemy soldier to win?

What does war look like at the personal and national levels when your enemy will die—and kill—for a cause that's already lost?

In the Battle of Iwo Jima, the US Marines invading the island of Iwo Jima seemed like an unconquerable force arriving in overwhelming numbers. Defending the island were Japanese soldiers with an invincible fighting spirit and invisible fortifications. Iwo Jima was a "perfect" battle: expected by both sides and fought over a well-defined area—military force against military force in a barren landscape, with no civilians to complicate matters.

It was appalling.

I have been acquainted with Mr. Bill Hudson for as long as I can remember, have lived in many of the same places (Los Alamos, Cornell University, and Puerto Rico), and have participated in many of the same activities (running, swimming, officer training, and the military). Only in the last few years have I learned what he did on an island I've never been to, more than twenty years before I was born.

Imagining how differently history would have gone if Japan had not surrendered in 1945, I wonder whether I would have been born at all. I wonder whether Americans now are prepared to fight the kind of enemy Hudson fought.

I want to present Hudson's story to young people, people who are the age he was in World War II. I hope they will learn, from a man with a deep understanding of war, what war is like and what war requires.

Karen Jo Tallentire
2014

Note on Terminology

It is normal for men in wartime to refer to the enemy by a one-syllable word, because combat is a time to say, "Watch out for that Jap!" rather than "Pay attention to what is going on with regard to that Japanese soldier!"

Also, when trying to kill another man, fighting words are used; if they weren't fighting words before, the tone of voice will take care of that. Often such words remain fighting words in peacetime, but not always. During the Civil War, for instance, southerners didn't call northerners "Yanks" out of affection; yet just a few decades later, Americans from North and South were calling themselves "Yanks," to say that the Yanks are coming over there, to Europe to fight for the British—who were the ones to come up with the name to begin with.

If the term "Jap" seems offensive, there is a reason: there was a war going on, and that was the term used for the enemy.

1

The Unseen Enemy

Monday, 19 February 1945

A chunky amphibious tractor circled around off the shore of Iwo Jima,[*] waiting for 0900: the appointed hour for the Marine Corps to invade the island. Nineteen-year-old Private Bill Hudson sat in the amtrac, watching ships two miles out shoot big guns at the island. Planes were dropping bombs. The island had been bombed for weeks. The Japanese holding the island couldn't have survived, but all the firepower still aimed at the island was heartening to see.

Hudson looked forward to this adventure. He knew men got killed in battle, but he had thought about what could happen and explained to himself why everything would be all right.

---

[*] Pronounced /ee-oo gee-mah/. Japanese does not accent syllables.

> I'm going to get killed, or I'm going to be alive. If
> I get killed, it won't make any difference. If I'm
> alive, that's pretty good. But then if I get wounded,
> it could be serious, or it could not be serious. Well,
> if I get wounded seriously, that's not so good. But if
> I get wounded not too bad—[1]

He had figured his odds of survival, and felt prepared.

He was well trained for landing on this island, and he was in a good unit. His officers were experienced from other Pacific battles. Hudson was confident they knew what they were doing. He was in the Fourth Division, scheduled to land on the north end of the beach, move north, and then turn east. His battalion, 3/25, would attack the high ground, called the Quarry, above the East Boat Basin. Then the battalion would move up to the O-1 (Objective for Day 1) line, far inland.

The amtrac was full of supplies: cases of ammunition, five-gallon cans of water, and a big box of ponchos. Hudson knew what the ammunition and water were for, but wondered about the ponchos.

Then the Navy guns stopped. The time had come. Hudson's craft headed for Blue Beach Two, the end of the beach furthest from the island's active volcano, Mount Suribachi.[*] At 0902, the amtracs in the first wave hit the beach. Hudson's wave, landing second at 0912, was the first wave with troops.[†] Wave after wave followed, each a few hundred yards apart.

---

[*] /soo-rih-bah-chee/
[†] The first wave carried such things as armored gun-bearing amtracs.

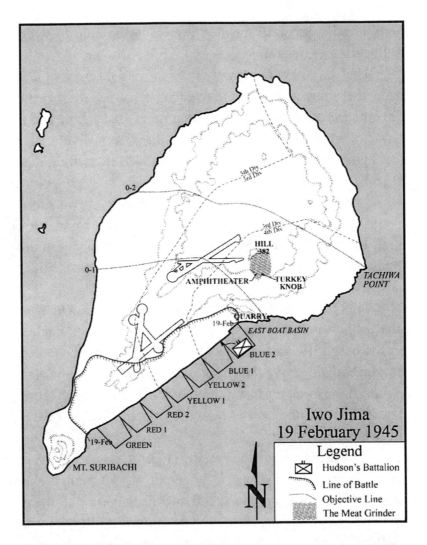

Ready for his first battle, Hudson jumped out as soon as he felt the thud of the amtrac going up on the beach. A mortar shell landed several feet away and hit his platoon sergeant, Mike Schrock, and his corporal and assistant rifleman. Overall, though, the island was quiet—just a bit of small arms fire that caused no major damage. The Marines were prepared to take some small arms fire while landing two-thirds of their force on the beach over the course of just one hour. If all went well, maybe they would be able to walk right across the island.

Hudson knew exactly what to do. He threw supplies from the amtrac on the black volcanic ash of the beach. Then he looked for cover, but found none. Instead, he had a series of sand terraces, each one a wall of sand five or ten feet high. The coarse pebbles of sand rolled underfoot, and he sank to his ankles.

Beach sand was the Marines' first enemy at Iwo Jima. Upon landing, vehicles sank to their hubcaps in sand, creating traffic jams, and Marines carrying fifty to one hundred twenty pounds of equipment sank to their ankles, calves, or knees.

Silent and hidden, Japanese General Tadamichi Kuribayashi[*] watched as wave after wave of Marines landed on the beach. He had chosen the landing area as the target for guns dug in above the beach on both sides and now was waiting for his target to be filled with Marines. The more he could kill on the beach, the more effective would be the other traps he had set.

Struggling across the beach, Hudson saw a big flare go up in the sky, and, as he later put it, "all Hell broke loose."[2] The flare was the signal for the Japanese to open up with everything they had. Every mortar, artillery piece, machine gun, and soldier with a rifle zeroed in on the Marines. Every part of the beach was a target.

> I never heard so much noise or saw so much smoke in my life. The scene could only be described as chaos, havoc, destruction, carnage, suffering, and death. That was an experience that was just absolutely unbelievable.

---

[*] /tah-dah-mee-chee koo-ree-bah-yah-shee/

The bombardment that followed destroyed boats, ships, and men. Moving forward through Japanese fire was the only way off the beach, and some Marines never made it *onto* the beach. Looking back at the waves of Marines that landed behind him, Hudson saw landing craft that had taken direct hits before the men could get out of them. All around him was noise, chaos, fear, uncertainty, and Marines being wounded and killed.

The noise was deafening, and the beach was full of smoke, devastation, wounded, mangled, and dead Marines. It was the most horrible sight I had ever seen in my life. To this day, I don't know how I got off that beach without being killed or wounded.

Now that death was all around Hudson, mind games didn't help anymore. Every second counted for survival. His brain concentrated on staying alive; it was hard to remember anything else. There was nothing he could do but tell himself, "I was told to get off this beach,"[3] and try to keep moving in. He kept moving, and the firing got heavier the further he went.

To get off the beach, Hudson knew his unit was supposed to move inland and off to the right flank, hugging a high cliff that should partly protect them from enemy fire. But there were pillboxes in front of them and machine guns and artillery were dug into the cliff. The enemy was firing from the Quarry they were supposed to take. Finding little cover, the unit got hit hard. Hudson crawled into a hole that was hot from a shell that had landed there seconds before he did.

The pre-invasion bombing hadn't wiped out the Japanese, but at least the bombs had exploded the mines on the beach and dug craters that gave Marines cover from most of the shooting. But a crater could be another trap. The Japanese would wait until several Marines were in a crater, then aim at the crater. One round could take out everybody in a direct hit.

Beach landings weren't new to the Marines. On a previous island, Peleliu, the Marines had learned how and why to get off a beach. As John McManus put it in his book *Grunts: Inside the American Infantry Combat Experience, World War II Through Iraq*,

> Frightened men asked corporals, sergeants, or lieutenants what to do and the leaders told them, thus giving them a job to focus on rather than their natural fear. The leaders understood that the situation was horrifying but not all that complicated. Staying on the beach meant death. So the best thing to do was move forward to destroy whatever, or whoever, was in the way.[4]

Although surrounded by chaos and carnage, the men went forward. As one Marine said, according to Haynes and Warren in *Lions of Iwo Jima*, "You've got to keep busy or you'll go nuts!"[5] They didn't go nuts. On the day of the invasion, only a third of one percent of the men were evacuated for combat fatigue. Men trained as Marines feared failing to do their parts more than they feared dying.[6]

The Marines could try to move forward, but how could they destroy invisible Japanese? The whole first day, Hudson never saw his enemy, only dead and wounded Marines. He could hear machine guns. He knew the Japanese had mortars, artillery, and rifles. But the fire was coming from caves and tunnels out of sight. With no targets to shoot at, he didn't use much ammunition. Never seeing the enemy—even dead—shredded morale.

> This was the devastating part of it; we didn't know what to shoot at, how to defend ourselves. And I didn't know that we had lost all of our officers so quickly. I didn't know that for a long time. Everybody was pretty much scrounging for themselves to find a place that was safe—if there was such a place.[7]

Hudson's battalion commander, Lieutenant Colonel Justice "Jumping Joe" Chambers, commanding battalion 3/25, took notes for his personal diary as he watched Hudson's company—K Company—go ashore. The casualties started right away with the wounding of Tom Witherspoon, the company commander. The executive officer, John Camien, took command and brought the company up the first terrace. Camien lasted about ten minutes.

Targeting of the officers continued, and by the end of the day, all seven of the officers K Company had landed with were dead or wounded.

Chambers noted that Hudson's company was in an especially difficult position. There wasn't room for the three companies of the battalion to land beside each other, and the battalion made a better target while turning. One company got separated, and Hudson's company had to move across behind another company as the Japanese started firing with everything they had. A tank battalion behind them drew enemy fire. The Japanese had a clear view of Hudson's company, and if they needed more observers, other Japanese were looking down from Mount Suribachi.

Single shooters hidden on Iwo Jima were often called snipers, though they didn't have to be marksmen with so many Marines so close. One of them killed Hudson's platoon leader, Second Lieutenant Charles Johnson. Hudson was beside Johnson. "I pulled him over to where I was, in a little depression on the beach. I could see he was dead, and that was the first time I'd ever been close to a guy who was dead. I realized he didn't need his .45 anymore."[8] Hudson took the Colt .45 caliber pistol and used it as a backup for his Browning Automatic Rifle (BAR).

Platoons tried to care for their dead and wounded, but often didn't know what to do with them. Hudson learned the ponchos he had seen were for covering dead bodies. "After the first day, it was obvious that we didn't have enough ponchos." There was no place to put a dead body out of the way. A wounded man couldn't be evacuated, because nobody was going back to the ships. Marines lined up their wounded on the beach, where many were hit again while waiting for a ship to come get them. Some Marines later listed as missing were literally missing. A direct hit left nothing to identify.

Marines still landing fought both rough seas and falling shells. The bombardment created a gigantic traffic jam as men struggling through sand died and vehicles were shattered, blocking the path of Marines still landing. Hudson thought himself lucky to have been in the first wave, since he got farther in.

The 3/25 battalion started out confused and wasn't given time to stop and sort things out. The deadly firing on the beach wouldn't end until somebody took the Quarry. Colonel Chambers, a big man wearing a shoulder holster and accompanied by a radioman and eight bodyguards, led his 3/25 battalion up the cliffs toward the Quarry, telling them to get up there before the Japanese did.

At one point during the effort to take the cliffs, the strafing from close air support was too close, almost into the Marine lines. Close air support was supposed to help the attack by strafing the enemy—if pilots could tell which ones were the enemy. The Marines had long bands of yellow linoleum cloth to lay on the front lines, showing pilots where they could start shooting. Hudson saw one Marine standing up waving the yellow cloth, trying to protect his unit by telling the pilots, "Hey, we're here,"[9] but meanwhile making himself an excellent target to the Japanese. Hudson thought he was "a pretty brave guy."[10]

Rain began, and it kept raining for the next couple of days. "We were soaking wet. The only thing that was dry was the top of my head when I kept my helmet on."[11]

The battalion took the Quarry, enduring deadly fire from the Japanese that shredded the battalion. Yet the effort finally stopped the firing on the rest of the beach. Battalion commander Chambers eventually received the Medal of Honor for what the battalion accomplished that day.

By 1800 hours, or 6 p.m., the battalion of four hundred men was reduced to one hundred fifty.

> The first day was just absolutely devastating, mentally and physically. Because there was no order as far as, 'Okay, my platoon, we're doing this.' We didn't know. . . . I think the word was, 'Find some secure hole, dig in, and hold on.' Because we couldn't go much further.[12]

Disorganized without their dead or wounded leaders and frustrated at not being able to see their attackers, the platoon members tried to protect themselves in what little cover there was. They prepared for a night attack, but the Japanese stayed quiet that night.

On the islands of Saipan and Tinian, the Japanese had made "banzai" charges—a tactic named for the Japanese patriotic battle cry. Banzaiing was usually suicidal, a last-resort attempt to turn the tide of battle or die. On Saipan and Tinian, the tactic failed; American forces had a solid defensive line that wiped out the Japanese. But in the chaos of Iwo Jima, with scattered groups of survivors trying to figure out what was going on, Hudson thought a banzai charge that first night "would have driven us back into the sea and the battle would have been a disaster for us."

Kuribayashi, however, was not ready to commit suicide. He had many other traps to spring. For now, nighttime allowed the Marines a chance to regroup and set up a defensive perimeter.

Nighttime was their first chance to organize since leaving the amtrac. "It was then when our platoon got together, and to see only twenty-seven men out of the original forty-seven was a hard thing to take." Even worse, the company overall had only sixty-seven men left of the two hundred fifty-five who had landed that morning. The others were dead or wounded. In a shock to their already fading morale, they realized moving in a few hundred yards had cost three quarters of their company. Like the Marines' plan of attack, Hudson's attitude didn't survive the first day. "Oh, my Lord, what is going on here? This isn't the way it's supposed to be."[13]

Morale—the confidence that a fight is worth fighting—is everything to an army. An army without morale is already defeated. Though the Marines were well prepared and invading with three times the forces of the Japanese, their morale was in shreds from the shock of sudden attack from an unseen and seemingly indestructible enemy who wasn't supposed to still be there.

The costliest invasion of the Pacific War had landed. Considering thirty thousand Marines were ashore, the 2,420 casualties, of which 501 were killed, might not seem a huge number. But the percent of damage was much higher for some battalions, such as Hudson's; and the destruction, confusion, and demoralization were so great the dead weren't counted yet. In fact, the numbers would not be known for several days. The Marines were nowhere near the line they were supposed to have reached that day. More than one thousand Marines of the Fourth Division were already evacuated to hospital ships. Landing boats, tanks, half-tracks, amtracs, cranes, and bulldozers were wrecked, crippled, smashed, and overturned. The debris around the beach was so thick that landing craft could land in only a few places.

In Hudson's platoon alone, out of forty-seven men, casualties included the platoon lieutenant, a group leader, a Navy corpsman, three other Marines who were dead, and the platoon sergeant who was hit by a mortar shell on landing. Another Marine was wounded by a mortar shell, one Marine lost an eye, one lost two fingers, and two more were wounded in other ways. Hudson's "best and closest buddy" was killed. At least he had somehow managed to kill two of the enemy first.

And all of this on a single day.

Some historians report the gunfire never slowed that night. But according to Hudson, the intensive shelling eased up after dark when much of the Japanese artillery stopped firing to keep their muzzle flashes from giving their positions away.

The titanic battle was only beginning. This Pacific War was a different fight from the one in Europe. After the invasion of France on June 6, 1944, the beaches of France were secure; a picnic could have been held on the beach that same evening. But Iwo Jima's beach stayed a target for a month. This was not an enemy who made a noble effort, then surrendered when further struggle was hopeless. This was an enemy who could be stopped only by death, whose only options were victory or extermination. The Marines had a terrible task ahead of them.

Hudson had not seen the enemy, but he had gotten his wish; he had seen action, more than many career Marines.[*]

---

[*]Combat time by the time the American flag was raised on Mount Suribachi added up to more close combat than the average professional soldier sees in a decade, according to Haynes and Warren, *Lions of Iwo Jima*, 161.

2

A Marine Grows in Manhattan

Generations of Hudsons have fought in various branches of the military. Bill Hudson's great-grandfather, a Civil War veteran, was alive when Hudson was born. Hudson's father was a New York City policeman and World War I veteran. His World War I service mainly involved shoveling coal in the Navy, but the senior Hudson liked Navy work better than farm work, and after the war he lived in Manhattan, far from a farm.

Between the world wars, the Marine Corps had a reputation from the World War I battle of Belleau Wood that appealed to many boys. The Marines, facing confusion and heavy casualties, had kept fighting and won both the battle and the nickname "Devil Dogs." Born and raised in peacetime, young William Hudson, Jr. admired the Marine Corps. Marines were tough, which was good, because he wanted to fight.

Hudsons in the Military

Civil War	Robert Jefferson Hudson (*great-grandfather*)	Confederate Army
WWI	William Alonzo Hudson (*father*)	US Navy
WWII	William Alfred Hudson	US Marines
1947-1948	Robert James Hudson (*brother*)	US Army
1969-1973	William James Hudson (*son*)	US Navy
1981-1987	Ty Manon Hudson (*son*)	US Marines

The streets of upper Manhattan seemed to Hudson a wonderful place to live in the early 1940s. He could take the subway downtown to see a stage show or big band. A movie cost a dime and a hot dog cost a nickel. Hudson was on the swimming team, did gymnastics on the high bars and parallel bars of public parks, and played lots of games he and his friends arranged.

Though Hudson was a member of a gang, he called it a "very good gang,"[14] not the sort for which New York City was infamous. The gang was interested in athletics, and none of them ended up in jail. Hudson did not smoke or drink.

When war started in Europe, most Americans weren't very concerned; America had decided after World War I that Europe should solve its own problems. Then, on 7 December 1941, Americans heard Hawaii's Pearl Harbor had been attacked. ("Pearl Who?" was one reaction, since

Hawaii was not a state yet.) The attack sank twenty-one ships and killed over two thousand people. The loss was not a crushing blow to the United States, but it was serious; sinking or damaging twenty-one US Navy ships in one strike was a major victory.

Japan was already occupying parts of China and Korea and was planning to expand further. The United States wanted Japan to stop but wasn't ready to declare war over the issue; after World War I, most Americans didn't want to fight other countries' wars. Japan thought if the US Navy

---

Global Domination

In late 1941 and early 1942, the whole Pacific seemed to be falling to Japan.

- Hong Kong and the Philippines: Fell within a month of Pearl Harbor. Thousands of American and Filipinos died on the Bataan Death March.
- New Guinea: Fell in March 1942.
- Indonesia: Fell in March 1942.
- India: Almost fell in early 1942.
- Australia: City of Darwin bombed in February 1942 while Australian troops were deployed in Africa.
- Korea: Occupied since 1910.
- China: Partly occupied.
- Pearl Harbor: Still paralyzed.

While Japan controlled much of the Pacific, occupied China, and threatened India and Australia, Germany threatened Russia. A glance at the globe showed Germany and Japan reaching toward each other across Asia, about to control half the world.

were crippled, Japan would have a free hand to do what it wanted and America couldn't and wouldn't do much in response. But the tactic backfired. The Pearl Harbor bombing infuriated Americans, especially because Japan's declaration of war came after the attack. Suddenly, this was America's war, and Americans had no doubt about whether they should be fighting. Japan had started the war; clearly, America should finish it.

Hudson, only sixteen, heard about Pearl Harbor after a football game. He thought the war would be over before he was old enough to fight.

The Tide Turns

- Doolittle Raid, 18 April 1942: American bombs fell on Japan, showing Americans—and Japanese—that Japan could be attacked directly, a huge morale booster for Americans. Most of the bombing crews landed in China and were smuggled out by the Chinese, though furious Japanese slaughtered whole villages for helping them.
- Battle of Midway, June 1942: The US broke Japanese codes, and Japan lost four aircraft carriers before retreating to save the rest. From Midway on, Japan defended a shrinking empire.
- Guadalcanal, 7 August 1942: Starting at Guadalcanal, US forces began taking back island after island from Japan, including the Gilbert, Marshall, Marianas, Caroline, and Solomon islands. Many islands gave their names to famous battles.

By December 1943, the US Navy could mostly move freely in what had been Japanese waters.

The Army, Navy, and Marine Corps started building up in the Pacific. (The Air Force was then known as the Army Air Corps.) Japan knew America would rebuild, but meanwhile, Japanese forces would have time to dig in around the Pacific.

US shipyards worked faster than Japan expected, turning out a destroyer in five months and a carrier in fifteen months. Engineers, inventors, generals, and admirals developed boats, landing vehicles, and strategies for what was called an "island-hopping campaign": a series of battles on Pacific islands to drive the Japanese back to Japan.

Hudson reached draftable age in 1943. "When I was eighteen, the war was still going on, so I realized that now I was in it." Volunteering for the Marines seemed better than being drafted by the Army.

Hudson's father wasn't so sure. From his own experience, he pointed out several advantages of the Navy: bunks with clean sheets, three hot meals a day, cool clean water, "and you may not get shot at."

Hudson still liked the Marine Corps better, and now that he had the chance, he wanted to try to get in. His father wished him luck and hoped the war would end soon.

Hudson wanted the war to be over too, but said, "I hope I can see some action after I enlist."

Joining the Marines was not a dramatic event. At the recruiting center, Hudson went to the line for joining the Marines. The recruiter looked Hudson over, talked a bit, and Hudson raised his hand. "And I was in."[15]

On 31 August 1943, Hudson entered boot camp at Parris Island, South Carolina. His hair was shaved off, he was given a uniform, he was lined up with the other recruits, and he was told how to behave. To Hudson, camp was "just a brand-new experience."[16] As they stood by their bunks on the first night, the drill sergeant warned them to get in bed and go to sleep as soon as he turned out the lights. In the morning, he said, after he called, everyone had better be standing by their bunks. He put a bucket of water in the middle of the barracks. At four in the morning, he returned and yelled, "Hit the deck!"[17] Most jumped to attention, including Hudson. A few didn't. The drill sergeant dumped the water on the sleepers, and they got up quickly. Morning was whenever the Marine Corps said it was.

Like Japanese samurai, Marines have a warrior tradition and code of behavior. Unlike samurai, Marines are made, not born, and come from every region and class in America. Boot camp showed Marine recruits what a Marine was and whether they measured up. Boot camp taught the self-discipline, spirit, integrity, confidence, and respect for authority critical for a Marine. Raw young civilians were transformed into men who could assume positions of honor and respect.

They were training for war and got news every day about what was going on in Europe and the Pacific. However, Hudson didn't follow war news; he was too busy. He did know that after Guadalcanal, a lot of the men returned with malaria. He heard about the enemy, about how "the dirty Japs were the enemy, and they fought dirty, and they did devious things. We were going to go kill Japs."[18] Boot camp taught Hudson that the job of Marines is to "take territory, break things, and kill people. If you can't do those three things, you better not be a Marine."[19] The recruits didn't have to enjoy their job, but they did have to be prepared to do it. This was wartime, and men sorted out any doubts they had about killing before joining the Marines. To hesitate over whether to kill the enemy was to be killed.

Boot camp was infamous for its Marine Corps drill instructors (DIs). They had a monumental job and a tight deadline—just ten weeks to make Marines out of seventy-five civilians. Being lovable was not part of the job description; DIs succeeded by being hated. In those days, DIs could and did shake and kick recruits, and they constantly abused the recruits verbally. But they never punched Hudson or his fellow recruits.

The training was physically and mentally intense. Having worked as a lifeguard the previous summer, Hudson had little difficulty with the physical challenges. He found the toughest thing was the mental discipline. "They try to break you down mentally, and they just demand things of you that are quite unreasonable."[20] But he understood the purpose. Fighting the DIs was no way to succeed at boot camp, and he went along with every order they gave. Hudson looked forward to the discipline of becoming a Marine. The DI, however hateful, was his buddy, on his team, making a Marine of him.

Punishments were creative in their cruelty, and though most of the treatment had a reason, some of it was just abuse. Once in the middle of September, which is very hot in South Carolina, the DIs closed the barrack doors and windows and made the recruits put on the heavy green overcoats they'd been issued. The recruits were told to crawl under one bunk and over the next, continuing until some passed out from the dehydration. "I think our DI got chewed out about this, because we never had to do it again." But the training had to be tough. The Marines were headed for something much worse than abuse.

If one man made a mistake, the whole platoon was punished. Fair or not, the platoon had to learn that in battle one man's mistake could hurt the whole platoon. In boot camp, the punishment was close-order drill with a locker box. That meant lifting a forty- to fifty-pound locker box that lacked handles, to the right shoulder. Then the DI would say "Left shoulder, arms," and they had to move the boxes to their left shoulders. Or, "Port, arms," and they had to hold the boxes straight out in front of them.

Many of their punishments resulted from the actions, or lack of action, of one recruit. Again, that was a lesson for the future. The group had to learn that since the actions of each affect all, one man could not be allowed to make the others suffer. Rather than go on punishing everybody for the actions of one, the DI gave the group permission to solve the problem of this one recruit themselves. He explained to the platoon that the guy might happen to "fall down the stairs" the next day. Of course, he would look beaten and bruised after that. If the DI were to ask, "What happened to you, private?"[21] he was to answer the DI, "I fell down the stairs."[22] "You guys understand that?"[23] asked the DI.

They did. A couple of them beat up the recruit and told him to shape up "because we're getting wiped out."[24] The next day the DI asked the bruised recruit what happened. "I fell down the stairs, sir."[25] Mission accomplished.

The DIs were tough authority figures with loud, raspy voices. "Don't look at me, boy. I ain't your mother. Don't look at me, boy. I don't love you. Keep your eyes straight ahead."[26] DIs could answer anything a recruit said or did with a sharp and salty response—such as the language used by the range master on noticing a recruit named Cannon on the rifle range. That unprintably poetic reaction gave Hudson his only laugh in ten weeks of boot camp.

Everybody had stories about the DIs. According to another Iwo Jima veteran,

One time they had us down eating grass, and the commanding general of the base drove by and stopped and backed up and asked the drill instructor what was he doing. He said, "Sir, they march like cattle, and I'm going to make them eat like cattle." The commanding general said, "Carry on," and drove away.[27]

As boot camp meant living in close quarters with strangers, things sometimes disappeared. If someone complained to a DI their socks got stolen off the line, the DI had a solution: "Well, you better steal somebody else's socks off the line, because in 1776 someone stole a pair of socks off the line, and it's been happening for the last 150 years."[28]

On Sundays they could go to church, although they weren't required to. Both Protestant and Catholic services were available, with Jewish services on Saturdays. On Sunday, recruits got to sleep an hour later and have a better breakfast.

Both the recruits' time and space were highly organized. They were occupied almost every minute of the day, except for a little time before lights out during which they could write home and do laundry. They had inspections every day, and even their socks and shoes in locker boxes had better be in the assigned places. Everything had to be kept more than clean. "You could eat off the floor of that barracks. It was clean. The toilets were like an operating room in a hospital. I mean, that was the cleanest place in the whole world."[29]

In those days, boot camp was ten weeks. Today, boot camp lasts longer, with more Marine Corps tradition and

U.S.S.R

Mongolia

Manchuria

Japan

China

Iwo
Jima

7. Guam August 1944 Marines
faced snipers in caves. Japanese
counterattack penetrated American
lines; even Marine cooks and clerks
used their rifles.

Burma

Philippines

Siam

French
Indo-China

9. Peleliu Fall 1944 Cost: 1,800
American and 11,000 Japanese lives.

4. New Britain Early 1944 Cut off
Japanese supply route to New Guinea,
preparing for U.S. invasion of the
Philippines.

Malaya

Dutch-East
-Indies

New
Guinea

8. Leyte Gulf October 1944 70 Japanese
warships, 716 aircraft vs. 166 American warships,
1,280 aircraft. Greatest naval battle yet, crushing
Japan's naval power. Cost: 2,900 Americans and
56,000 Japanese lives. Only 389 Japanese surrendered.

Australia

Approach to Iwo Jima

Alaska

10. Luzon January-July 1945 Invasion of the Philippines, largest US land campaign of the Pacific War.

5. Saipan June 1944 Cost: 3,400 American and 16,500 Japanese lives. Japan couldn't replace those men; America could. More disturbing yet were the civilian suicides by grenade or jumping off cliffs. Evidently the civilians feared death less than what the Japanese military told them the Americans would do.

6. Tinian July 1944 Cost: 200 American and 6,000 Japanese lives. This time, thousands of civilians ran for American lines after a loudspeaker assured them the Japanese military's warnings about the U.S. were false.

Hawaii

3. Kwajalein Early 1944 Japan fought savagely but vainly for this island, a Japanese possession since World War I

Marshall Islands

Pacific Ocean

1. Tarawa November 1943 One of the Marines' bloodiest fights of the Pacific campaign, costing 1,100 American lives in

2. Bougainville November 1943 Cut off the South Pacific center of Japanese airpower. As on Iwo Jima, Japanese fire on the beach surprised Marines.

Solomon Islands

Legend
■ Territory Held
▤ Territory Threatened

history incorporated into the training. In 1943, while making that history, the Marines focused on teaching recruits to shoot.

Practical rifle training meant taking apart a rifle and putting it back together blindfolded—and there had better not be parts left over. A Marine had to know his rifle inside and out in case it jammed. Rifle drill taught respect for the weapon, and the understanding that in battle life depends on care of the rifle. "One time somebody dropped a rifle, and that's the ultimate horror—to drop a rifle."[30]

When inspecting rifles, the DI always found something wrong. Even if the weapon was perfect, he never said "Good job." He always found something negative to say to show recruits they weren't, and couldn't be, perfect. If the butt of the rifle was on the ground, he'd pick it up and look at it and say, "There's dirt, there's dust on the butt."[31] But if a recruit rested the rifle on the lip of his sole to keep the butt off the ground, he'd be told, "You did not have this rifle in the right position."[32] Recruits couldn't win. The point was to learn to submit to authority, reasonable or not, because the middle of battle is no place to argue.

Hudson learned to field strip and reassemble an M-1 rifle in seconds. He shot "Expert" on the rifle range, and thought that was "pretty good for a New York City boy who had never shot a rifle before."

Boot camp also involved learning to march and perform close-order drill. Marching is not just showing off. Marching is practice in paying attention, moving with precision, obeying orders, and trusting commands without knowing their purpose. The squad going left finally rejoins the squad going right—if both obey the commands. Hudson was absolutely amazed that at the commands "Left flank, march; right flank, march; to the rear, march," seventy men marching down the road would all turn at once, taking pride in their precision. In ten weeks, the Marine Corps had the recruits passing in review before their officers, demonstrating their new skills in a military parade.

Hudson also learned to throw grenades, shoot a carbine, perform hand-to-hand combat, use a bayonet, and go through drills wearing a gas mask. As a former life guard, he easily passed the Marine swim test. By the end of boot camp, he knew that 10 November, the Marine Corps birthday, was more important than any other day of the year. At the end of boot camp, his attitude, ability, and shooting earned him the rank of Private First Class (PFC). "The most important day in boot camp for me was when my platoon marched across the parade grounds on the last day and the DI shook my hand and called me a Marine."

Not every man who entered boot camp came out a Marine. Those who did weren't perfect; some weren't even courageous. But the Marines were a team, their lives depended on one another, and they made history together. The new Marines put aside their daily khaki and green uniforms to get their pictures taken in borrowed dress blue uniforms, presenting a good image of the Marine Corps for the folks back home. In some cases, those pictures were the last that families would have of their sons.

There was one last boot camp tradition to fulfill: scaring the next bunch of recruits. The new Marines yelled at the new arrivals, "You'll be sorrrry!"[33]

Now PFC Hudson was a real Marine, ready to fight— and headed for a desk job, as his good score on an aptitude test got him assigned to photogrammetry school. Out in the Pacific, Marines were dying: 423 at Bougainville; soon 950 more at Tarawa. Other places no one had ever heard of— Saipan, Tinian, Guam, Peleliu—were about to become the sites of famous battles.

From November 1943 to January 1944, as Marines bled and died in the Pacific, Bill Hudson sat in North Carolina making maps from aerial photographs. One day,

Private First Class Hudson in borrowed dress blues

To Jennifer,

Now you know what I did 70 years ago.

Semper Fi

Bill Hudson

he discussed his dissatisfaction with his buddy. "'Why did we join the Marine Corps?' He said, 'We joined the Marines to fight.' I said, 'Yeah, why are we doing this at our desks, drawing maps? Let's get out of this outfit.'"[34]

They requested a transfer, and Hudson ended up in demolition school. Explosions sounded much more exciting than maps. He learned about trinitrotoluene (TNT), dynamite, blasting caps, prima cord, a new explosive called composition C-2, and the use of satchel packs. Hudson enjoyed demolitions and finally felt he was doing something worthwhile for the war effort.

One event in demolition school was an endurance test in which Marines were kept awake and moving for sixty hours. The test involved hiking, climbing, paddling across a lake in a rubber boat, calisthenics, and other activities. They were allowed ten minutes every hour to sit down, but weren't allowed to lie down. Every six hours, they fired their rifles to see what effect fatigue had on their accuracy. The results had ominous implications for extended periods of combat. "I noticed that my shooting was not very good after the first twenty-four hours. The targets seem to spread apart and I thought I was seeing double." Hudson finished the test despite hallucinations near the end, for the prize of seventy-two hours off to see his family.

While Hudson finished demolition school, US forces took Kwajalein. The following spring, Hudson went through a new program, an underwater demolition school at Fort Pierce, Florida for men who were "half fish and half nuts." The school was demanding, with intensive training. In fact, it was Navy SEAL training in an early form. The new program was so important to the war effort that underwater demolition couldn't be mentioned in news stories.

Hudson and his fellow students practiced going ashore at night in rubber boats, scouting the beach to see what kind of obstacles there were, and destroying obstacles with the appropriate explosives and weapons.

It was the spring of 1944, and Marines in the Pacific were taking New Britain. In letters home, Hudson described life as a teenager in Marine training, preparing for a war too far away to imagine.

We were having a mellow time learning about diving, walkie-talkie radio sets and communications under water. We started our diving with a few lectures and demonstrations about the various diving suits and gear, etc. We learned about radios and underwater sets, etc. It sure was interesting dope and at first we went down in a pool that was only eight feet deep but it was fun. The Marines had a big advantage because we had diving for three days and had lots of time with it. Well, that night we went into the channel for some night diving. We went out from VP boats [short for LCVP or Landing Craft, Vehicle, Personnel: a flat-bottomed landing craft] and went over the side. We went down about sixty feet and just wandered around the bottom and keeping in contact with the man on top. Each of us were down for fifteen or twenty minutes and it is the loneliest feeling in the world. We had a light and our radio and that's all. You can see about five feet away and that's all . . . and you can hear your breathing going up and down like a dynamo. Every once in a while you get a check on the radio from the tender above. And it seems like you are down in another world all by yourself.

Hudson's diving equipment wasn't the scuba gear Jacques Cousteau made famous; in 1943, Cousteau was still developing that. What Hudson wore was a metal helmet with air hoses going up to the surface.

So far I have about three hours to my credit in the deep blue sea. We would get problems to do in the water, like cutting boards in half, locating objects that were tossed overboard, inspecting the bottoms of piers and docks and doing a lot of practical work that is really on the ball.

The training was dangerous—sitting in a boat with explosives and connecting charges, dodging flying concrete—but so was what Hudson was training for.

Instead of diving today we had a little demolition work and it was plenty of fun and action.

We were offshore by our destination and went off from the rubber boats—our crew was the scout crew and we had to go to shore and see what kind of obstacles we were going to get rid of, etc. The lieutenant picked me to swim to shore and get the dope and clothes and all from shoes to steel helmet. I dropped in the ocean and swam about one hundred yards to get the dope . . . . Returned OK safe and sound, we paddled back to our VPs for the explosives and the three marine crews went in for the business. It was just like the real business except we didn't have any supporting artillery fire or top fifty-caliber machine gun shooting at us. It was a race for time and we set our charges on concrete blocks in the surf three to each crew.

We were in the surf placing charges and getting ready to knock out the nine blocks. We use five twenty-pound packs of Tetratol on each block and we carry the explosives in our boats. We connected on our charges, etc., and all the necessary steps of demolition work, got out to a safe place and bingo, concrete was flying around like mosquitoes at night. We then paddled up to the beach again and cleared fifty yards of barbed wire and some other obstacles on the beach. Bingo. Bingo bang. It's all over—our mission is completed and we shove off for home. We got in about 3:00 p.m. and secured for the day. Our problem was completed very satisfactory and it was just a preliminary problem to next week when we are going to mess with the payoff course and work just like the real McCoy— from sunset to sunrise. All night work, just like demolition men do in combat. It's all surprise and our work has to be done when it is dark. We will have the days off next week so I'll be able to get plenty of sunshine and laying around on the beach. Next week we are going to combine everything we learned for actual demonstrating. VPs, mine sweeping, diving, explosives, obstacles, etc., etc., and more etc.: all on K or C rations. It should be terrific.

A tough Marine, skilled at finding things underwater at night and blowing them up as necessary, Hudson nevertheless sounded a bit homesick. Wishing he were headed for war in Europe, so he might have a chance of seeing his family while passing through New York City, he mourned, "It sure would be terrific if the marines ended up in the Atlantic but the chances are one in a million. We are strictly Jap bait not Jerry stuff." Either way, "Things look like we are shoving off after the payoff course is over." He would be leaving his home continent shortly.

As usual we had another night payoff course again last night. It was just about on the same scale as the other problems. Out in VPs, launch the rubber boats into the water send in a scout, which is always me, and get the lowdown on what's to be blown, etc. We didn't have much trouble last night at all. The ocean was pretty calm and we handled our boats fine. We blew up steel girders in the water, concrete blocks, tank traps, barbed wire and pill boxes. It was all done simulating actual combat maneuvers and we were all quiet, fast and low all the time. We made with the noise and blew all our objects clear and made the usual reconnaissance to see if it was all completed and well enough to land LSTs and LCM and troops—it was fine and dandy so off we fled back home . . . .

Tonight by luck is our last night problem and it is going to be the payoff of the payoff—in plain English it is going to be a lulu and a half. We are going to have a lot of navy brass and braid watching the spectacle and watching us work. Of course they will all flee when the charges go off but they will still be on hand to watch us. Tonight we are going to work with 3 army engineer crews also. So with 6 crews we can really be able to do a good job.

A poem Hudson wrote in marching cadence:

My Life in the Marine Corps

Hudson

In August nineteen forty three
A boot marine, that was me
A quick time hike, the bayonet course
Some rifle fire, a DI boss
Two months of hell the time did fly
I lived somehow, yes I got by
A ten-day leave—a PFC
To Camp Lejeune Photogrammetry
Pencil pushing—unracked brains
Not too well off; not much gains
A quick transfer. Engineers
Had no time to go bang ears
Demolition with lots of noise
A trip to Florida with heap hep boys
Lots of action lots of water
Everything from boats to mortar
Three weeks standby with lots of doubt
But it was true, we're shipping out
To California without a loss
The rugged 5th Amphibious Force
Of future life I cannot say
But I'm making history today. Amen.

End

It was June 1944. In Europe, Allied troops landed in Normandy. Marines who would land on Iwo Jima with Hudson now fought on Saipan. PFC Bill Hudson, just another lifeguard a year ago, was part of the first Marine Corps Underwater Demolition Team, crossing the United States by train to ship out from Treasure Island, California.

From California, the first stop was Pearl Harbor, where Hudson saw some of the damage done three years before. The war started to seem real. Hudson headed west across the International Date Line, but kept missing the action he had joined the Marines to see.

> We landed at Saipan, in the Marianas Islands, but the fighting was over. We were told that we were supposed to blow up the beach on Tinian Island; we arrived too late and the 5th Amphibious Reconnaissance Battalion did the job that we were supposed to do.

Hudson crossed the International Date Line three times before seeing combat. And then his underwater demolition training went to waste, right before one of the most celebrated uses of underwater demolition occurred at Iwo Jima, the day before the invasion.

The purpose of demolition was to prepare beaches for assault waves of invading Marines. Before the Iwo Jima invasion, Lt. Col Whitman S. Bartley writes in *Iwo Jima: Amphibious Epic*, underwater demolition swimmers, working "under heavier mortar and small-arms fire than they had ever before experienced" landed the day before the main force with the mission of,

> [C]hecking beach and surf conditions, searching for obstacles on the beach, and in the water

approaches. Obstacles were to be destroyed when found. Some of the swimmers actually crawled out of the water to collect soil samples for examination on board ship.[35]

Gunboats accompanied the swimmers, and the Japanese fired on the gunboats, thinking the boats were the main landing. The eight gunboats were lost, along with forty-three lives. The event was a serious loss for US forces but a tactical mistake for the Japanese, as the big Japanese guns were unmasked and US forces were able to put most of them out of commission. If the guns had fired on the actual invasion, far more than forty-three lives would have been lost.

Instead of swimming to Iwo Jima through ocean waves, Hudson landed the following day with a rifle in the assault waves; between the Marianas Islands and Iwo Jima, his Marine Underwater Demolition Team had been broken up and merged into the Fourth Marine Division to replace casualties from Saipan and Tinian.

Hudson was upset. The Marine Corps wasn't. "They gave me a BAR and said, 'Now you're going to be in an infantry platoon.' I said, 'Well, I've had demolition training.' The guy said, 'Well, if we ever need it, we'll know how to use it.'"[36]

With the Fourth Division, Hudson headed back to Hawaii, for more training on the island of Maui. Instead of a romantic Hawaiian beach, Maui meant a thirteen-mile super obstacle course through the Haleakalā* Crater, a jungle training center, a village-fighting course, a cave-fighting course, and an infiltration course. The Fourth practiced landings and foxholes, studied Japanese weapons,

_____

* /ha-lee-AH-kuh-lah/

learned about booby traps and mines, and practiced codes and communication. Hudson tried his BAR and liked the big, solid weapon. He learned to take it apart and clean it. With the BAR set on automatic and a magazine in it, Hudson could shoot twenty rounds in a couple of seconds. "That was a lot of firepower. . . . So I was just resigned to the fact that I wasn't in underwater demolition anymore; I was now in the infantry."[37]

V-mail saved wartime shipping space; letters were copied onto microfilm for transport.

Hudson learned the concept of *esprit de corps*—the camaraderie and pride in a unit that allows two Marines to tell each other that the Marine Corps stinks and then beat up a Navy guy for saying so. "I felt very much a part of 'The Fighting Fourth,' and was accepted by them as a fellow Marine." Coming from combat veterans, acceptance was no small honor to a new Marine. Another Iwo Jima veteran said the level of comradeship was such that he felt he would rather die than knowingly let down his fellow Marine.[38]

Hudson's unit practiced teamwork and tactics, the members coming to know themselves and one another very well. If the lieutenant said to go, the unit would go. The guys on Hudson's right and left would be there, he knew, covering him. Hudson's company was given tasks such as night attacks on another company to see if they could steal a machine gun or a tent. Sometimes the tasks were fun and games, but they were always practice, and they usually seemed to be just another maneuver, "marching up and down on Maui—in the rain."[39]

Monday, 22 January 1945

Sun Tzu was a Chinese general who lived several centuries before Christ. In his world-famous manual on warfare, *The Art of War*, he compared the irresistible strength of a conquering force to waters bursting into a deep chasm. Four weeks ahead of the invasion date, the division set sail, a force bursting toward Iwo Jima.*

Hudson didn't know where they were going. He had never heard of Iwo Jima. He did know they were going into

---

* LSMs and LSTs sailed 22 January, the transports with the main body of the division left 27 January.

combat on an island, but not Japan yet. When the division was safely away from the range of any radio communication, the Marines were told the name of the island where they were headed. Iwo Jima is still hard to find on a map; it is a speck of land in the middle of the Pacific. It was then an unknown lump of rock, sand, a couple of airfields, and an abandoned village.

Iwo Jima means "Sulfur Island." The island had been a sulfur mine, and mining tunnels pierced it. Trees had grown on the island, but they had been cut down to reinforce the caves, and there was a clear field of fire. Weeks of bombing had left the island bare, black, and rocky. "If there was a hell on earth, that was it. It was a desolate rock. It had no grass, no trees, no towns, no civilian population. It was a fortress, and it was Japanese homeland."[40]

Hudson's battalion commander, "Jumpin' Joe" Chambers, showed them on a relief map the beach they would land on. The island was shaped like a pork chop, with Mount Suribachi on its southern tip. North of that tip was a narrow neck with beaches on either side. Big ships couldn't anchor near shore, so Marines and cargo would land in smaller craft.

Chambers told the battalion how well fortified the island was, but explained that the operation would probably be short because the Navy had been bombing the island for more than two months. The battle was to be fought by the Marine Corps' Third, Fourth, and Fifth Divisions. The plan was to land on the eastern beach and sweep across the island while securing the airfield. Chambers showed the battalion which side of the beach they would land on, and the airfield they would take as their first objective. Then, he said, they would take the rest of the island. The Marines planned to spend a week or two taking Iwo Jima and then head to Okinawa.

The goal of the fighting was to take the only airfield between the Mariana Islands and Japan. Whichever side held Iwo Jima held a great advantage. Sun Tzu called such places contentious ground:[41] ground that attracts battle. Because of B-29s, Iwo Jima was literally to die for.

The B-29 crews flying to Japan had a dangerous job. The B-29 Superfortress improved on the B-17 with twice

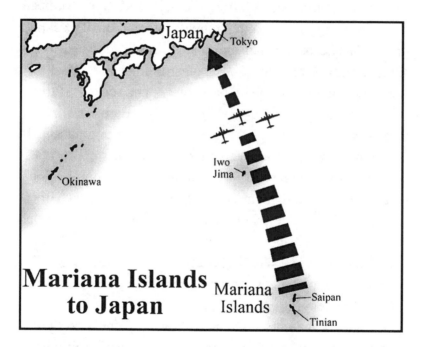

the bomb payload, fifty miles per hour more speed, and half again the range—3,250 miles. The crew of eleven could really take the war to Japan. But the B-29 was new, untested by combat, and still called the three-billion-dollar gamble. By August 1944, the Mariana Islands were in American hands, and American bombers started launching from there to bomb Japan, since there was no place near Japan to launch aircraft. A B-29 had to fly from the Mariana Islands fourteen hundred miles north to Tokyo, drop bombs, get shot at, and fly fourteen hundred miles back—if the engines worked, if the weather didn't turn bad, and if Japanese fighters didn't shoot down the aircraft. For that sixteen-hour flight, the aircraft had fifteen minutes to an hour's worth of spare fuel.

Iwo Jima lay beneath the flight path, halfway there; detouring around the island wasted precious fuel. Japanese fighter planes from Iwo Jima attacked the B-29s. They also sent Tokyo warning to prepare for the bombers, so the B-29s met antiaircraft fire if they reached Japan.

If the bombers survived their battle damage, they faced Iwo Jima fighters again on the return trip, hundreds of lonely miles before the nearest friendly airstrip. Under Japanese management, an Iwo Jima landing was not an option. B-29 crews captured by the Japanese could expect to be shot, bayoneted, beheaded, burned alive, scalded, or given to medical professors to be experimented on until dead.

Ditching the aircraft at sea was less certain death. Along the route, destroyers and submarines watched for downed aircrew. But when Amelia Earhart had disappeared over the Pacific Ocean seven years earlier, four million dollars hadn't found her. Nobody would spend that kind of money in wartime on a missing B-29 pilot.

The B-29s had only been in use in the Pacific for about nine months, but before the Marines took Iwo Jima, seventy-seven of them had already been lost, with their aircrews of over eight hundred men. The US factories couldn't replace aircraft that quickly, and pilots were threatening not to fly the missions anymore. Americans tried bombing Iwo Jima, but the Japanese quickly repaired the airstrips.

Iwo Jima had to be taken in order to turn Japan's early warning system into an American safety net. In September 1944, Admiral Nimitz got approval to take the island.

The Japanese understood Iwo Jima's value to America. Japanese Navy Captain Tsunezo Wachi,[*] garrison commander of the island before Kuribayashi arrived, knew that,

> If we could totally defend the island, we could break the U.S. plan to attack the mainland by B-29's. On the other hand, if the U.S. seized the island and made use of it, the mainland would be an easy prey to B-29's. Therefore, it was imperative for us to defend it by all means.[42]

Furthermore, Iwo Jima was historically and traditionally part of Japan, and a place where Japanese people had lived. Though far from Japan, the island was nowhere near anywhere else, and nobody else had wanted it until now. The island was the gateway to Japan. If Iwo Jima fell, the enemy would enter the gate over the dead bodies of Japanese warriors. That would be the beginning of the end: Japan would no longer be fighting for victory, only honorable death. Iwo Jima was so vital that one Japanese major suggested sinking the island to keep it out of enemy hands, if such a thing were possible.[†]

During four weeks' travel to Iwo Jima, Hudson's unit had little to do but plan and practice for combat. Daily, they

---

[*] /tsoo-neh-zoh wah-chee/

[†] "Major Y. Horie voiced this plan as follows: 'Now we have no fleet and no air forces. If American forces will assault this island it will fall into their hands in 1 month. Therefore it is absolutely necessary not to let the enemy use this island. The best plan is to sink this island into the sea or cut the island in half. At least we must endeavour to sink the first airfield.'" Bartley, *Iwo Jima: Amphibious Epic*, 7.

shot their weapons out from the deck into the ocean. They cleaned their weapons and kept them fully loaded.

Hudson didn't worry about the battle. "I almost looked forward to it. But I think I was very ignorant about really what it was going to be."[43] Battle seemed just one more adventure, following the adventures of boot camp and demolition training. "I thought, 'We're going to do what we're going to do. We're going to kill Japs, and we're going to take that island.' There was no doubt in my mind that we weren't going to take it."[44] Unable to foresee the battle, Hudson felt no apprehension.

On the day scheduled for invasion, the Marines were ready with weapons, cartridge belts, and bayonets. (Hudson's BAR did not come with a bayonet.) Each had a solid chocolate D ration bar, two canteens, and a helmet. Before the landing, each Marine got sprayed all over with DDT "to keep from getting bubonic plague or something, I guess."[45]

On 19 February 1945, after the traditional pre-combat breakfast of steak and eggs, Hudson and 20 or 30 other Marines entered their amtrac down in the tank deck of the ship and waited for the signal to start the last two miles over the sea to Iwo Jima. "A sailor on deck yelled down to us and said, 'You guys will be back for noon chow. There ain't no Japs alive on that island.' Boy, was he wrong."

3

Understanding the Evils of War

*During World War II, if you didn't mature fast, you
were dead.*
—Paul Tibbets, pilot of the Enola Gay[46]

Tuesday, 20 February 1945

The first day on Iwo Jima had been a one-sided fight with an invisible enemy. The real fight was still to come, not on the beach but on the main island. On this second day, the rain continued and the sea got rough, increasing the difficulty of landing anything. Landing craft kept coming in, trying to bring food, water, and more men, but the beach was still a traffic jam of wrecked and stalled equipment, so space for landing was hard to find. Tanks trying to move inland got stopped by minefields and rugged ground.

Slowly, everyday life on Iwo Jima took shape as Marines moved off the beach, found out who was left and where they were, and gradually got food and supplies moving inland past the sand. Hudson's platoon got "some degree of order and organization,"[47] he recalls. They found the volcanic rock inland was better than the black sand. "That black sand was amazing to walk on. You went right up to your ankles in it. You couldn't dig in it; it just was soft."[48]

Hudson was only a couple hundred yards inland, and the beach was still "getting pounded every hour."[49] The Regimental Combat Team (RCT) 25 that Hudson was part of gained less than two hundred yards in most places during this second full day of combat. Then, topping off the day, RCT 25 got hit by a friendly fire air strike. Close air support was coming in, and with fifteen thousand men per square mile[50] fighting over this tiny island, mistakes happened.

RCT 25 was a unit under the Fourth Division that fought mostly on the right-hand side of the division. Within RCT 25, Hudson was in the Third Battalion (called 3/25). His battalion was commanded by Lieutenant Colonel Justice M. Chambers, who had led the battalion in taking the Quarry the previous afternoon.

Within the battalion, Hudson was in K Company, the one whose landing difficulties Colonel Chambers had commented on. The company had an attached artillery unit, which was supposed to be behind the infantry, supporting them, with a forward observer ahead to tell the artillery where to shoot. But the artillery had been devastated the first day along with everything else. Even after the artillery unit was functioning, Hudson didn't have much faith in artillery that was shooting at targets it couldn't see.

Within K Company, Hudson was in the second platoon, which had started out with forty-seven men. His identification was "Private First Class William Hudson, 3-K-25"—that is, "Third Battalion, K Company, Regimental Combat Team 25." He was one man in a platoon in a company in a battalion in a regimental combat team in a division that had the job of taking the right-hand side of Iwo Jima. The veterans of the Fourth Division had taught Hudson to be proud of his unit at every level, and at every level that spirit was essential for enduring what was to come.

Since all the officers had been killed or wounded in the first few hours of battle, Hudson's sergeant, Manuel Martinez, led the platoon. Martinez had appointed himself leader for lack of anyone with higher rank, and also because he was a natural leader who knew what he was doing. Martinez was from New Mexico. He was a veteran of the Fourth Division who had fought in every beachhead operation so far; Iwo Jima was his fifth.

According to Hudson, Martinez was lucky not to get shot, because "he did some very dangerous things to save our lives,"[51] including scouting the area at night, when Marines were supposed to stay in their foxholes and shoot anything that moved. Martinez did tell the platoon that he was going, but night was a time to shoot first and identify later.

On his scouting trips, Martinez gained valuable information: he found Japanese emplacements and caves, and was able to tell the platoon what it needed to do the next day. Martinez was not completely helpless out there either; he knew how to use his weapon, and he shot a lot of Japanese. Hudson regarded him as a hero.

Colonel Chambers, explaining in his memoirs how heroism was so common it wasn't even surprising, noted that Martinez once walked erect into a cave full of trapped Japanese soldiers and killed 15 while escaping unscathed.

Hudson's explanation of Martinez's survival was luck and a lot of smarts. Hudson felt he himself was very lucky; he was in the right place at the right time, not in a sniper's sights, not below a falling mortar shell, not in front of a spraying machine gun.

The first couple of days, you could have been the smartest guy in the world, and you could have got hit with a mortar shell. No way you could have avoided that . . . the beach was the target, and if you were on the beach you were part of the target.[52]

The Japanese were shooting into a grid where all the Marines were; they couldn't miss.

Hudson was certainly lucky, but, in the informed opinion of other Marines, he too was smart.[*] He was promoted accordingly; after the first week, Hudson's sergeant put him in charge of a squad. A few months later, the Marine Corps would try to educate him as an officer.

There was great heroism on Iwo Jima, where uncommon valor was common, but these descriptions can mislead a generation raised on movies. War rarely has the drama of a film. A combat team of movie heroes would soon be dead, because battle requires caution. For a team to survive, most of its the men have to do their duty without doing anything too crazy. But the team must also move, and there isn't much motion if each man only does his duty.

---

[*] It was a credit to Hudson that he survived carrying a BAR. The BAR's bipod was distinctive and anyone carrying a BAR attracted unfavorable attention from the Japanese, according to PFC Bernard Link of I company, 3rd Battalion, Landing Team 3/28. Haynes and Warren, *Lions of Iwo Jima*, 118.

Someone has to be aggressive, ignoring his own safety, daring others to move forward. The others call these men crazy, which might be the case. Or they might be real heroes, fighting for something greater than themselves. Whatever the motivation, these men set the team standard for courage, and they set the pace.

For a unit to win a battle yet live to fight again takes that combination of caution and daring.

Wednesday, 21 February 1945

Some Marines never saw a Japanese soldier on Iwo Jima, though they certainly saw their effects. Hudson saw many Japanese soldiers, but not until the third day or so. That was the time someone pointed out Japanese bodies lying on the ground, and at those words, a Japanese soldier in front of Hudson got up and started to run. Trained for this moment, Hudson shot him. Then another started to run, and the group shot him. It happened so fast that only afterward did they realize they had shot somebody for the first time. For all their training, all their certainty that shooting was the right thing to do and had to be done, there was always the question: in a real battle, do I have the courage? Now Hudson had gained confidence in his weapon and in himself to do the job.

> I felt good about it. I know you're not supposed to feel good shooting somebody, but I felt good about killing someone that was shooting at me. . . . I actually knew that I shot that guy and killed him, and I was glad I did it. And I knew I could do it.[53]

Pretending to be dead while hiding a weapon was a common Japanese guerrilla tactic. Marines learned not to trust even dead Japanese. Another tactic was to leave live grenades beneath dead bodies, or call for help like a wounded Marine, then shoot the unarmed medic who came. Throughout the battle, whenever they could, the Japanese hid their dead so Marines would only see dead Marines. These tactics ("dirty tricks") made Marines glad to kill Japanese, and tempted Marines to torture them, but there wasn't time. The Marines needed to get across Iwo Jima and on to Okinawa. Japanese standing in the way had to be killed, but torture was rare.

Killing the enemy released frustration at what was happening to fellow Marines. From an action report on Iwo Jima quoted in *Iwo Jima: Amphibious Epic* by Lt Col Whitman S. Bartley: "Occasionally the tanks flushed out enemy personnel who could be killed by the infantry. This always raised the morale."[54] Yet good feelings about killing did not automatically create bloodthirsty butchers. Another veteran, quoted in Larry Smith's *Iwo Jima: World War II Veterans Remember the Greatest Battle of the Pacific*, showed more resentment for critics at home than for the enemy he shot, reflecting that,

> [W]hether I or somebody else did it, I kinda thought maybe I did it, but then it's nothing to brag about, taking a man's life. They was there just like we were, probably didn't know any more than we did. Anyway, that's life, that's the way wars are. People that know everything ain't in the war. They're sittin' back somewhere.[55]

Few Japanese were taken prisoner, because doing so was difficult. Unless they were shell-shocked, Japanese soldiers usually killed themselves first. If captured, they begged to be shot; surrendering was both illegal and a shame to the soldier's family and ancestors. Of the twenty-two thousand Japanese on the island, all three Marine divisions together took only 216 prisoners. Over sixty of these were not even Japanese; they were Korean slaves, who weren't so eager to die for Japan. "We didn't take many prisoners. . . . I never had a chance to capture any. If I was that close to them, I shot them."[56]

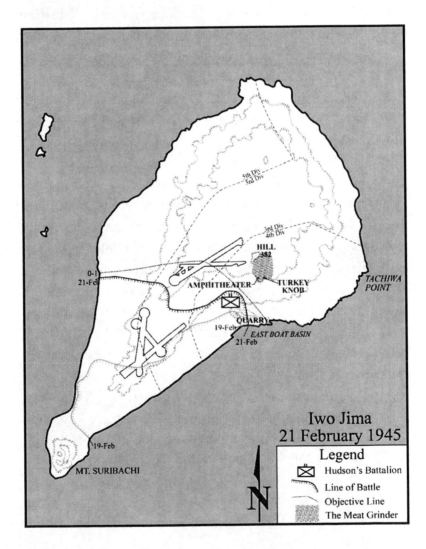

Iwo Jima
21 February 1945

Legend

⊠   Hudson's Battalion

  Line of Battle

  Objective Line

  The Meat Grinder

Instead of being killed immediately after surrender as they expected, Japanese prisoners eventually got food, water, and clothing better than they'd had before. In return, they cooperated very well with American intelligence officers trying to find out where Japanese forces were hidden, where there were mines, and what the plans were. The prisoners would tell everything they knew. One reason for this complete attitude change was the Japanese respect for the victor, a relic left over from the samurai Bushido code. The victor won everything; the defeated gave up his own way of life to follow the victor. Japanese prisoners no longer considered themselves Japanese. A belief equating surrender with slavery would inspire a man to fight desperately, and suicide could certainly look better than surrender.

Another part of Japanese belief was in the divinity of Emperor Hirohito. The soldier, as a mere man, was to obey the emperor, not to question whether the war was successful or even useful. Since nobody wants to give unpleasant information to divine personages, Hirohito may not have known enough to bear much responsibility for the war. He did not seem to be as militaristic as the men surrounding and advising him; we do know of his great interest in marine biology. If born to another family, he might have spent his life studying science. Still, the authority to stop the war was his.

On this third day of battle, Chambers's battalion was kept in reserve until midafternoon, then moved through heavy enemy fire to fill a gap between the other two battalions. The 100-250 yards gained this day meant finally driving the enemy off the cliff heights and Quarry area. The Marines had taken the area on the first day, but there had still been Japanese around, shooting at the beach. With those shooters gone, Marines landing were no longer under fire from the high ground.[*]

Colonel Chambers had said before the battle, "Anybody who doesn't like combat is crazy. I'm going to get the Medal of Honor if I have to kill every man in this battalion to get it."[57] The battalion must have thought he really was trying to get them killed as they struggled to take the cliffs and Quarry. But a gradual, cautious approach would mean more Marines landing on the beach being killed. Without the fighting spirit of Chambers and the men who followed him, the well-protected Japanese position overlooking the beach, intact despite weeks of bombing, would have kept on killing.

At night, the enemy attacked, and enemy fire continued—not only on the front lines, but also on the beaches and rear areas.

The depth of Iwo Jima's defenses was becoming evident. A cutaway view of Iwo Jima would show the Japanese were *in* Iwo Jima, not on it. In natural caves of rock soft enough to be excavated by hand tools, the Japanese cut tunnels big enough to run through upright while holding weapons. The Japanese had dug an underground network with more than 750 gun emplacements, five-foot-thick concrete blockhouses, and—under Mount Suribachi—a complete hospital and four stories of tunnels.

A thousand pillboxes encrusted the sides of the volcano. The caves were at least five feet wide and high and thirty-five feet deep, with protective angled entrances. The diggings protected most of the Japanese from most of the pre-battle bombing. As they dug (in ground temperatures of up to one hundred twenty degrees, on rations of a biscuit

_____

[*] The recommendation for Chambers's Medal of Honor said that capturing this high ground was essential to the invasion's success.

and a cup of water per day), the Japanese hid the dirt they excavated, probably dumping it in the sea at night, so watching American planes and ships had no idea that the Japanese were burrowing into the whole island.

Caves were a good place for tanks, which were otherwise not very useful on the rough ground of Iwo Jima. A Navy destroyer escort was surprised on the day before the landing when it came close to the beach and got hit by a gun that came out of a cave, shot, and pulled back in again. Looking at their maps, the Navy found no gun emplacements recorded in that area. The gun turned out to be a tank parked underground, an emplacement invisible to American forces scanning or flying over the island to gather information.

As the Marines moved inland, the tunnels, caves, and crevices left them confused about where the enemy was and how many there were. When Marines approached, the Japanese could shoot, disappear through the tunnels, and then reappear behind the Marines. Once in a while, Marines could shoot their enemy from a distance; usually they had to get near a cave to shoot inside. While they approached, they would probably be shot at from nearby—or connect-ed—caves.

While Japanese tactics forced Marines into close-range fighting, the Marines did their best to stay as far back as they could. Hudson knew not to enter a cave to see whether everyone was dead. "I don't think we were warned, but we knew we weren't going to go in. I was never going in. Nobody was. We knew we'd blow the cave up rather than going in. Going in would be pretty dumb."[58] If the Japanese weren't dead, whoever went in would be.

Marines moving inland figured out how to blow up caves and tunnels, killing everyone inside without having to go in. They also sealed caves with bulldozers, but if the cave was actually a tunnel, the Japanese could come around and shoot the Marines who had just tried to entomb them.

Marine tools of war included fragmentation and white phosphorus grenades as well as satchel packs—little packs full of explosive. A pill box or machine gun nest might require a bazooka team. If the men could get close enough to use it, a flamethrower would ignite a jet of jellied gasoline known as napalm, burning anyone in the way and sucking up all the oxygen in the enclosed space. For a cave, Hudson would shoot his BAR inside to keep anyone from coming out, clearing the way so one of his men could crawl up alongside and throw a grenade. "I would fire into it a couple of times. Nobody would come out."[59] After the grenade went off, the men watched for phosphorus gas escaping from air holes. If there were air holes big enough, the Japanese might escape through them.

The military genius behind Iwo Jima's defenses was Tadamichi Kuribayashi, a general descended from generations of samurai, who had visited the US and knew his enemy. He thought war with America was a bad idea. Still, he fought brilliantly and died for his emperor, winning the respect of friend and foe.

In Manchuria, Kuribayashi and many of his men were part of the army that committed crimes against prisoners of war and civilians. Their military opponents had been poorly trained and organized. Now, on Iwo Jima, the same army faced serious combat against well-armed, well-trained Marines. Kuribayashi, if not all his men, realized their battle was hopeless. Kuribayashi knew America was coming with overwhelming forces and Japan was running out of everything. He knew he would not be resupplied and knew he could not hold Iwo Jima. But he understood the purpose for which the doomed force fought: to buy time for Tokyo to

Value of Human Life

Japanese soldiers did not value their own lives in comparison to serving Japan, and they thought any non-Japanese, especially those who had opposed Japan, were worth even less. In return, those who experienced Japanese inhumane treatment usually didn't value the Japanese as fellow humans.

In the devastated Chinese city of Nanking in 1937-38, the Japanese army killed half the surviving populace, mostly civilians, in the "Rape of Nanking." Exact counts are impossible in a devastated city, but this slaughter of about three hundred thousand people probably killed as many Chinese as the total number of Japanese who later died in Hiroshima, Nagasaki, and the firebombing of Tokyo.*

In Hong Kong, the soldiers bayoneted hospital patients and raped nurses and nuns. In Guadalcanal, prisoners of the Japanese were vivisected, while prisoners on ships from the Philippines were allowed to drown in excrement.

In Manchuria, the Japanese army did experiments: How long before a person dies if injected with this, or if that is cut off? The experiments were conducted on civilians and prisoners, including infants, the elderly, and pregnant women.

About a third of US Army prisoners of Japan died in captivity during the war, compared to only one percent of US Army prisoners of Germany. But Asian civilians under the Japanese died in far greater numbers. Civilian Asian deaths in 1945 alone were twice the number of American battle deaths during the entire war. In 1945, civilians in Asia were dying at the rate of over, and probably far over, one hundred thousand per month due to the war.

---

*Estimating 80,000-120,000 deaths in Tokyo, 70,000-120,000 in Hiroshima, 35,000-60,000 in Nagasaki, for a total of 185,000-300,000 Japanese deaths. The low and high estimates for Nanking deaths are 260,000 and 350,000. These figures are from Iris Chang, *The Rape of Nanking: The Forgotten Holocaust of World War II* (New York: Penguin Books, 1998), 6.

prepare Japan and the Japanese to fight the coming American invasion.

Certain death was no reason to quit. Surrender, which would bring extreme dishonor on one's family, was impossible. So Kuribayashi prepared to die with honor, spent months planning traps for Marines, and issued "The Iwo Jima Courageous Battle Vows," saying:

> Above all else we shall dedicate ourselves and our entire strength to the defense of this island.
>
> We shall grasp bombs, charge the enemy tanks, and destroy them.
>
> We shall infiltrate into the midst of the enemy and annihilate them.
>
> With every salvo we will, without fail, kill the enemy.
>
> Each man will make it his duty to kill ten enemy before dying.
>
> Until we are destroyed to the last man, we shall harass the enemy by guerilla tactics.[60]

"Grasping bombs" made more sense than using tanks on Iwo Jima. The rough, volcanic terrain forced the battle into man-to-man encounters fought with personal weapons such as guns, knives, and grenades instead of distance weapons such as artillery, tanks, and mines. Stepping over a crack or rounding a corner, a Marine might find himself face to face with the enemy. The first to shoot won.

Hudson's equipment during the battle included his BAR, a knife called a Kabar, plenty of ammunition (a full cartridge belt plus a bandolier of magazines for the BAR), two canteens of water, two grenades, a gas mask, chocolate D ration bars, his camera, and an entrenching tool (the Marine Corps term for a shovel). Instead of a knapsack, he threw his gas mask away after the first day and used the case to keep hand grenades, a Japanese battle flag, and other souvenirs. He also had, wrapped up in the gas mask case, $100 from a bet he had won by diving thirty feet off a ship at night, and he carried the money throughout the battle. "I was more worried about that . . . $100 than I was worried about getting killed."[61] He asked a sergeant to send it to his mother if he died.

The BAR impressed Hudson with its power, and he used it every day he was on the front lines. Though he heard of men who shot their own finger or foot to get out of the fight, he was not tempted to try. He knew the BAR would have blown his leg off. Besides, shooting himself would be abandoning his unit, and Hudson wasn't going to do that.

Hudson made good use of grenades. American grenades came in two kinds: fragmentary and white phosphorus. The American fragmentary grenade had square-inch pieces of shrapnel. "When that went off, it got everybody in the vicinity."[62] The white phosphorus grenades contained burning phosphorus, which could burn a hole through anyone it landed on.

Hudson decided grenades were the favorite method of the Japanese for committing suicide.

> They would shoot at you all day, and if they ran out of ammunition they would take a grenade and hit themselves on the helmet with the grenade to detonate it, stick it in their belly, bend over, and blow themselves up.[63]

Considering suicide an honorable way to avoid capture and gain the approval of their ancestors led to a very high suicide rate among the Japanese. Bending over a grenade held to the abdomen not only increased chances of fatal damage but also reflected samurai suicide methods, which were based on the belief that the spirit resides in the abdomen. Hudson was not impressed with a belief that caused soldiers to destroy themselves, calling it "military malarkey,"[64] and considering allegiance to what he called "the stern code of Bushido" in the Courageous Battle Vows to be fanatical.

The mortar was not a personal weapon, but it was the worst weapon the Marines experienced on the beach. Shells dug themselves into the sand and didn't explode far sideways. But mortars, which didn't dig in, would wound or kill anyone within forty-five feet.

One mortar the Japanese fired from a deep cave had a 240mm shell that looked like a fifty-gallon drum flying through the air, a garbage can full of explosives going end over end. The Marines called it the "screaming mimi," "floating ash-can," or "bubbly-wubbly." The first few fired didn't even land on the island, and the Marines laughed at the inaccurate weapon. As the aim improved, they stopped laughing. The mortar was usually fired at night, with a terrible noise, and though it remained inaccurate, wherever the shell landed, it blew a hole bigger than a twenty-five-yard swimming pool. "It was unbelievable,"[65] Hudson said. Eventually, the Marines found the launching cave, and the mortar quit firing. Japanese prisoners later said setting off this mortar had been as scary as being on its receiving end.

Thursday, 22 February 1945

The fourth morning of battle brought cold, drizzling rain. The surf almost stopped evacuation of casualties. But Chambers's battalion moved to a slightly better position and could see to shoot more than two hundred enemy driven from hiding places by rockets. This was one of the largest groups of Japanese yet seen, at about one percent of Iwo Jima's Japanese forces. That afternoon, Colonel Chambers was severely wounded.

For what he and his battalion did over these four days, Chambers received the Medal of Honor and his second Purple Heart. Chambers's Medal of Honor citation says,

> His zealous fighting spirit undiminished despite terrific casualties and the loss of most of his key officers, he again reorganized his troops for renewed attack against the enemy's main line of resistance and was directing the fire of the rocket platoon when he fell, critically wounded.[66]

Hudson's version of the wounding is plainer:

> We were lying around one day, and he came up and said, "You've got to move out." Someone yelled to him, "There's a sniper firing through there." Chambers said, "Let's go get him." He went up, and he got shot with a bullet. He almost died. He didn't die, but he got hit bad .... He wasn't very smart going through where someone just told him there was a sniper.[67]

Yet Hudson called him "a real leader; he was a tough Marine."[68] As a private, Hudson knew the colonel only from a distance, but he respected him. "I think everyone respected him as a leader. We knew we had a good battalion commander."[69]

To Hudson, it was obvious the colonel should have changed plans in response to a known threat. Japanese thinking was different, Hudson discovered; there were times the Japanese would walk right into a known threat. At one bunker that Hudson's unit attacked, a Japanese soldier ran out and they shot him about ten yards out. A few seconds later, another ran out and also got shot. Another followed him. Three or four ran out in the same place, got shot, and died in the same place, which Hudson thought was kind of dumb. American soldiers would have gone a different direction after the first one got shot.

Afterward, they found the first one was an officer. The officer had presumably told the others to follow him, and they had.

> That's when I realized the obedience of the Japanese soldiers to their officers, obedience to their deaths. I learned something that day when we killed four Japanese soldiers.[70] When they were told something, they did it. That was their way of life.

On the flag Hudson took from the helmet of a Japanese soldier he shot was writing that translated as: "You have to be honored, loyal, and beat the enemy to repay the Emperor, to be loyal and good for your country."[71]

Unquestioning obedience is a powerful weapon, easily destroying undisciplined enemies—if used wisely. There is a difficult balance between good discipline and letting the man on the scene think for himself. A commander, seeing what a front-line soldier can't, might have to order the soldier to do something that looks crazy from the front lines. The soldier must trust the commander while understanding the commander doesn't know everything; he has

Rosenthal's picture of Marines raising the flag over Mount Suriba-chi inspired many works of art, including the Iwo Jima Memorial statue near Arlington National Cemetery.

to keep watching for changes the commander couldn't know about.

Japanese discipline impressed the Marines. The Japanese were good, they said, though Marines were better. Both Marines and Japanese were well-trained warriors, but with important differences. Marines could criticize or disagree with their leaders, and their leaders backed them up with supplies and artillery. Japanese leaders left their soldiers on Iwo Jima without hope of resupply or rescue, expecting them to keep fighting without question.

Friday, 23 February 1945

On this fifth day of battle, the Fifth Division raised the flag on top of Mount Suribachi. A second flag raising, of a replacement flag, was caught on film by photographer Joe Rosenthal and became one of the most famous pictures of the twentieth century.

Hudson was elsewhere at the time. He thinks he remembers seeing the flag being raised on Suribachi, but a flag on the mountain didn't stop his fight, halfway across the island. "[W]e had three weeks to go before that island was secured."[72]

The beach slowly cleared; supply and evacuation worked better. The battered RCT 25 was ordered back behind the lines, though "behind the lines" on this tiny island meant nothing to artillery fire and hidden Japanese. The platoon lost several men this day. Hudson's platoon guide was shot in the chest; another Marine got hit in the ankle; one was taken out for combat fatigue ("went nutty as a fruitcake") and another for shell shock. Shell shock is a physical effect on the brain after a nearby explosion. Men with combat fatigue act much like men with shell shock without necessarily having being near explosions.[73] Combat fatigue, also called battle fatigue syndrome and combat stress reaction, is hard to define. Combat fatigue isn't the same as, but can lead to, post-traumatic stress disorder (PTSD). The condition can look like cowardice or weakness, but is seen even in men who received the Medal of Honor. Combat fatigue seems to be related to how intense the fighting is compared to what the mind can accept. Iwo Jima was intense compared to almost anything.

Hudson became familiar with the condition:

They'd shake. They'd make dumb statements, like one guy . . . wanted to make a phone call to call his mother. He walked away. They would do things that were completely irrational. They would cry. They would call for their mothers.[74]

Some went to hospitals. Some recovered easily, but for others recovery took a long time. Hudson never came close to "cracking up" on Iwo Jima, and thought he was strong enough he never would. Decades later, he isn't so sure. "I thought I could handle it all, and I evidently did handle it all there. I'm not handling it all too good right now. It's amazing. Sixty years later I'm still mentally involved."[75]

Another Marine's description of 23 February said that by this time the terrain looked like the moon because of all the bomb craters, and the wind made the volcanic ash feel like buckshot in their faces. The fighting was hand-to-hand, chasing and being chased by Japanese in trenches. They fought grenade duels and often found themselves coming around the far side of a Japanese pillbox that was fighting from the near side.

After five days, Hudson's unit had moved maybe a third of the distance they would eventually travel across the island. Their front line was close to the points they were supposed to have reached the first day. By now, they were supposed to have been finishing up this battle; nobody had expected its ferocity and severity. The Marines remained sure they would win, but "eventually" was the only word to describe when. All their strength, courage, training, and tactics weren't getting them across the island on schedule. They settled into a routine of shooting and blowing up things during the day and protecting themselves from the Japanese at night. Still ahead of the Marines lay steaming volcanic terrain and the Meat Grinder.

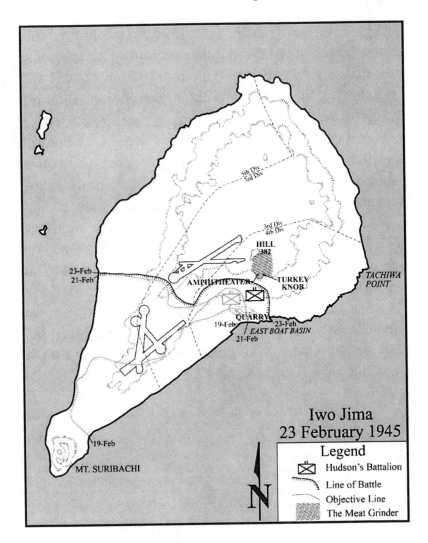

Iwo Jima
23 February 1945

Legend

Hudson's Battalion
Line of Battle
Objective Line
The Meat Grinder

Between the first few days of combat and his last day, events on Iwo Jima are cloudy in Hudson's memory. Lack of sleep alone probably affected his memory, as the stages of sleep the Marines missed were the ones that would have built the neural connections necessary to retain memories. In addition to the lack of sleep, stress—from constant noise, mortal fear, deaths of friends, and destruction—helped confuse events. Also, the men were in almost the same place doing much the same thing for about four

weeks; one day was much like another. So most of the following details about the position of Hudson's unit come
more from division histories than from Hudson's notes.

On Iwo Jima, Hudson went so far as to question his
choice of the Marine Corps. One day, somewhere in the
middle of the battle, Hudson was in his foxhole and looked
out at the ships offshore. He thought about the sailors
sleeping in their bunks and eating three hot meals a day.
Remembering his father's advice, he decided, "Gee, my old
man was pretty smart after all."[76] But then a kamikaze
plane hit one of the aircraft carrier tenders. There was no
safe place in this battle. Hudson concluded, "If I had to do
it all over again, I still would have joined the Corps."

Sun Tzu, the ancient Chinese military expert, said that
only those who understand the evils of war understand the
best way to fight.[77] Iwo Jima was making Private First
Class Hudson an expert on fighting.

4

Routine Combat

Hudson got used to life in combat; it became a routine. Instead of excitement or euphoria, he felt a developing confidence in himself as the days went on. Rather than a constant bombardment, the battle had turned into a series of one-on-one duels. The job was now, "the guy in that hole was shooting at me, and I had to blow his hole up before he got me and my squad."[78] Hudson told himself, "I'm not going to get killed. I know what to do now."[79] He felt he understood how the Japanese operated, what this battle was all about, and how to handle combat. He decided, "I'm going to make this."[80]

Hudson was not callous or numb to the fact of death, but he was able to compartmentalize the event as something that happens in combat. "And I'm here now, and I'm part of what combat is all about, and it's going to be over soon, and we'll get out of here."[81] He knew that after the battle, they would return to Maui, where they could rest without being shot at every night or having mortar shells dropped on them. "There was a beginning, there was a middle, and there was an end. We didn't know when the end would be. If you got hit, that would be it maybe."[82] Hudson felt he became immune to, not hardened by, combat. "I mean, I don't relish the thought of seeing a dead body or somebody getting shot. I adapted to it, because it was reality. It happened, and it can't be changed."[83]

Another Iwo Jima veteran said,

> It's hard to explain, I'm afraid, for it's difficult to imagine battle without thinking of heroics and dramatics, of dashing figures and climactic spectacles. It's even difficult for me to do now, when I have seen that it's not like that. It's like work. It is work . . . .And the only feelings evident are those of tiredness and anger, and, when a mission has been handled with a minimum of loss, grim satisfaction.[84]

Saturday, 24 February 1945

On this sixth day of battle, there were more losses in the platoon. Hudson's squad leader was hit in the leg, a Marine in his platoon "cracked up" after five straight days of rain, and another was transferred to the company command post.

The Fourth Division faced an area called the Meat Grinder where, north of the beaches, a rocky plateau full of caves and canyons hid the core of the Japanese forces. The Fourth Division was the meat. The Meat Grinder's three teeth (Hill 382, Turkey Knob, and the Amphitheater) protected one another and had to be taken together or not at all.

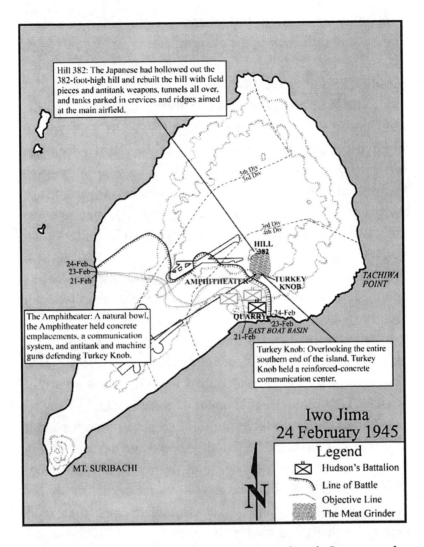

Hill 382: The Japanese had hollowed out the 382-foot-high hill and rebuilt the hill with field pieces and antitank weapons, tunnels all over, and tanks parked in crevices and ridges aimed at the main airfield.

The Amphitheater: A natural bowl, the Amphitheater held concrete emplacements, a communication system, and antitank and machine guns defending Turkey Knob.

Turkey Knob: Overlooking the entire southern end of the island, Turkey Knob held a reinforced-concrete communication center.

Iwo Jima
24 February 1945

Legend
Hudson's Battalion
Line of Battle
Objective Line
The Meat Grinder

To take the Meat Grinder was to break Japanese defense and communication, but the Meat Grinder was the bitterest and most costly part of the Battle of Iwo Jima.[85]

Over several frustrating days, Marines captured Hill 382 almost every time they attacked, but each time the Japanese moved out and started firing at the Hill, driving the Marines back. When the Marines left, the Japanese returned. Likewise, the Marines would charge the

Amphitheater easily in the morning, fight bitterly all day, and have to pull back in the evening.

Sunday, 25 February 1945

The Fourth Division gained about one hundred yards, but Hudson wasn't in the heavy fighting, as RCT 25 stayed in Division reserve. Perhaps this was the day Hudson described when his unit was pulled back in reserve to give them a little rest. "Reserve was only about 100 yards from the front lines, but we felt reasonably safe because we knew we had Marines in front of us." Still, a bullet could go 100 yards.

They were hungry enough for eight of them to eat as one meal a Ten-in-One Ration, a big box meant to feed ten men for a day—but whether it actually would depended on the men and the day. Besides the Ten-in-One Ration, they had K, C, and D Rations for food. K rations were survival rations, boxed food with a canned main dish and a variety of sides. C rations, the equivalent of today's Meal Ready to Eat (MRE), were portable pre-cooked substitutes for fresh food: cans of meat and vegetables, bread and dessert. D Rations were emergency food—high-nutrient chocolate bars. The Ten-in-One Ration was in a box or can like the K rations, but included things like scrambled eggs, meat and beans, spaghetti and meatballs, or beef stew. "[I]f you got spaghetti and meatballs, that was good. The powdered eggs were horrible—cold powdered eggs. The stew was pretty bad; a lot of fat would be on the top."[86]

The food was made to have a shelf life of years, and some of it was quite old. There were jokes about whether the food or its box tasted better. Though there was a variety of food, they ate it all cold; the Marines didn't make fires, so as not to draw gunfire. But in places, the volcanic ground could heat a buried can of C rations.

Sometimes an army gets cut off from supply lines and endures hunger and thirst, but Hudson never had to worry about being hungry. "That was the least of my problems."[87]

The Japanese attacked that night, and enemy shells fell in both front lines and rear areas. The shells' gunpowder was one of the constant smells associated with Iwo Jima. Another was the sulfur smell which came both from the sulfur mines all over the island and from Mount Suribachi's fumes.

Monday, 26 February 1945

After a week, the Japanese still held three-fifths of the island. RCT 25's job today: to attack the Amphitheater and Turkey Knob. Moving up behind a curtain of artillery fire, the men made one hundred yards, but whereas the Japanese had previously retreated under attack, they were now fighting to the death in their positions. Hudson's Battalion 3/25, the one that had been commanded by Colonel Chambers, had an easier day on the far right of the division, clearing the coast of Japanese troops just east of East Boat Basin. As usual, night meant Japanese trying to get into Marine lines, and mortar fire in front and rear areas.

As soon as the sun went down, the Marines would make a line of foxholes, two men to a hole. One man slept, and the other watched, then after an hour they would trade off. Hudson used his Colt .45 automatic to keep himself awake, moving it from one hand to the other, with the idea that as long as he kept the .45 moving, he wouldn't fall asleep. After his hour was up, he would wake the other man, give him the .45, and fall asleep immediately.

The Marines had grenades ready to throw if they thought there was some movement, but they did not fire their weapons at night. Rifle fire showed where it came from, giving the enemy something to shoot at. Grenades at night did not advertise the thrower's location.

Often only a few strands of concertina wire and twenty yards separated the Marine front lines from the Japanese and a possible night attack. Anyone leaving a foxhole risked being shot as an enemy, since thirsty Japanese soldiers searched for foxholes at night, looking for water and for throats to slit. Sometimes they would throw a grenade in a Marine foxhole. Other times they would jump in momentarily and stab one Marine, so the confused Marines would attack each other.

> The Japs used to yell at us at night to harass us or to find out our positions. They would yell things like "Hey Joe," and "Marines you die." If there was any humor about being in this battle, this was as close as it got.

One man in Hudson's platoon knew a bit of Japanese, so the Marines yelled back in Japanese some comments that were printable and others that weren't. "We learned phrases that meant, 'Take off your clothes, surrender, we will not murder you.' We wanted them to surrender."[88] The reason for removing clothes was to be sure the prisoner wasn't hiding a grenade or some other weapon, but the Marines would give the prisoner a helmet for protection. "So they'd be walking around with just a helmet on."[89]

Tuesday, 27 February 1945

The day started with forty-five minutes of artillery fire on the Japanese. RCT 25 kept beating against the Amphitheater, Turkey Knob, and the Japanese front lines down to the coast. Fighting out to the right of the Meat Grinder, Battalion 3/25 was able to gain two hundred yards and had to stop to stay in contact with the other battalions.

Casualties in Hudson's platoon for this day included one Marine who was knocked out for three hours by shell shock, another Marine hit, and a third, only seventeen years old, who lost his left arm.

> Any time a guy was hit, the first thing he yelled was, "Corpsman." .... The corpsman would come out of nowhere and run out, usually right in line where the guy got hit, and begin treating him immediately, right on the spot.[90]

Corpsmen were Navy, but wore Marine uniforms. They were trained to stop bleeding and treat battlefield wounds, but they saw horrible things they were never trained to handle. They did what they could, and at that time they were unarmed in the middle of combat, which was why Marines were particularly upset when Japanese shot corpsmen by impersonating wounded Marines. Five hundred corpsmen were killed on Iwo Jima, and many more wounded. "I think every Marine had respect for the corpsmen."[91]

Corpsmen treated wounds to help Marines survive long enough to reach more extensive treatment. If the Marines survived, behind the front lines there were even operating rooms, built by roofing empty Japanese cisterns or setting a pre-built plywood room in a hole and covering it with a tarpaulin. Though the distance from the front lines to battalion aid stations wasn't far, the terrain and enemy fire made it seem a long way.

Wednesday, 28 February 1945

Wednesday was mostly a replay of Tuesday, starting the morning with artillery fire. Again, Battalion 3/25 had to wait for the other battalions during the day. That night, however, most of the Japanese activity targeted 3/25.

By the end of the day, the Japanese still held Hill 382 and Turkey Knob, but the Meat Grinder's defense was worn down enough for the Marines to move ahead around

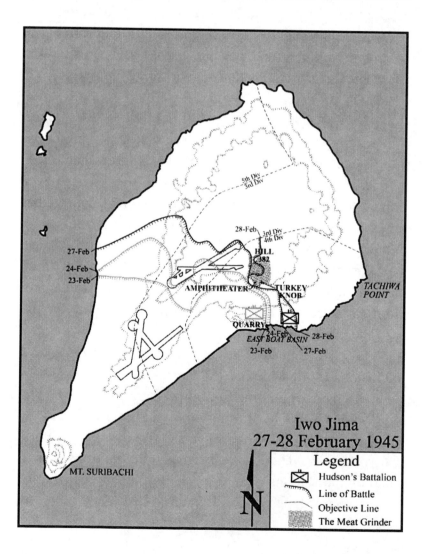

Iwo Jima
27-28 February 1945

Legend

Hudson's Battalion
Line of Battle
Objective Line
The Meat Grinder

its strong points, leaving islands of Japanese in a sea of Marines. The hill was outflanked, and the Marines were ready to bypass the Amphitheater and keep pushing east to the coast.

Thursday, 1 March 1945

RCT 25 tried to get rid of the bulge around the Amphitheater and Turkey Knob, but at day's end, they were right back in their morning position.

Friday, 2 March 1945

After so many bombs had moved so much dirt, terrain maps made before the invasion were fairly useless. On this eleventh day of battle and sixth straight day of fighting in the Meat Grinder, RCT 25 tried to surprise the Japanese by attacking Turkey Knob without firing artillery first. When the Japanese noticed them moving forward, RCT 25 poured fire into the blockhouse on top of Turkey Knob. The Japanese hung on. RCT 25 took heavy casualties and had to withdraw. Discouragingly, RCT 25 finished the day back in the position they had started from that morning. Battalion 3/25, on the far right, was supposed to hold its position, not attack, but sitting there getting hit by mortar fire was frustrating. Finally, in the afternoon, 3/25 got permission to move ahead. They quickly took three hundred yards and dug in on new ground for the night.

Saturday, 3 March 1945

On this day, the Marines broke the Meat Grinder. Late in the day, they were able to secure Hill 382, and now the Amphitheater was outflanked. Meanwhile, another unit relieved the worn-out RCT 25 and cut off the pocket of Japanese at Turkey Knob.

The Japanese defense was broken, but at great cost.
The Fourth Division had 6,591 casualties, 2,880 from the
Meat Grinder alone, and its men were exhausted.

Hudson's platoon lost a Marine who sprained his
knee, but later he returned and finished out the battle.

Hudson during the battle

Around this time, Hudson's unit was pulled off the line for
a few days, and someone took a picture of him wearing a
red necktie his mother had given him for Christmas. "I
wore it all through the battle. I guess it gave me good luck."
The handle of his Colt .45 is visible in the picture as well as

the toothbrush in his pocket that he used to clean his weapons.

Toothbrushes were not for teeth, though Hudson did brush his teeth during the battle at least once. One day the squad got a Red Cross package consisting of one toothbrush and two or three tubes of toothpaste.

> It was for the squad, so we brushed our teeth—all of us with the same toothbrush—and we didn't use anywhere near all the toothpaste. But we didn't confuse that toothbrush with the toothbrush that we all had to keep our weapons clean.[92]

The weapon-cleaning toothbrush was critical since weapons got "pretty cruddy,"[93] and whether a weapon worked when fired was a matter of life or death. The men cleaned their weapons every day and every night. "You wouldn't dare use somebody else's toothbrush for your weapon."[94]

Many matters of appearance and hygiene took second place to survival. During his time on Iwo Jima, Hudson never shaved and never changed his underwear, socks, or clothes. He had plenty of ammunition, water, and food (even if it was only K or C rations), and that was all he needed to do his job. Cigarettes were issued to the men; two or three came in a K ration box. Behind the lines, they may have smoked a lot, but Marines at the front were told not to smoke. "Lighting a cigarette at night would be a dead giveaway."[95] Anyone who smoked did so during the day. "I didn't smoke, so it never bothered me, and I don't remember being in a hole with anyone who did."[96] Hudson threw or gave away his cigarettes.

Sunday, 4 March 1945

Now that the Marines held the best ground, there was less Japanese artillery and rocket fire, but the Japanese fought individually from hundreds of rocky caves and crevices. The rest of the Fourth Division headed for the coast, swinging around RCT 25, which fought on the division's right for the rest of the battle.

The weather was gray and overcast for the first B-29 landing on Iwo Jima. A few American planes had already

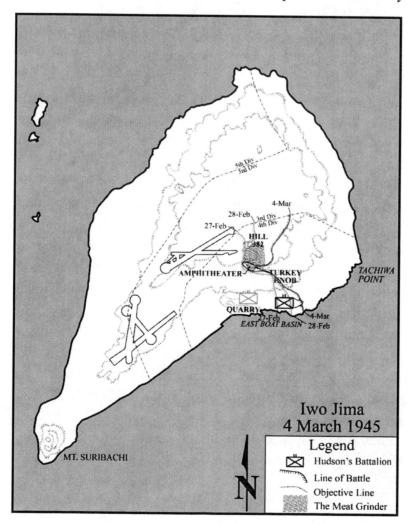

Iwo Jima
4 March 1945

landed on Iwo Jima, but what the Marines were fighting for was a safe haven for B-29s. The Japanese had been fiercely defending as much airstrip as they could even as the Fourth Division struggled past the Meat Grinder nearby. Engineers had worked on the Marine-held part of the airstrips since 24 February, stopping only at night or when enemy fire got too heavy. By 4 March, the Marines held enough of the main airstrip to give B-29s a better chance than landing in the ocean.

The runway was three thousand feet of dirt in the middle of a battle, with a windsock on a pole at one end and a jeep with a radio for a control tower. Fortunately, many pilots of that era were thrill-seekers who'd fallen in love with flying after seeing barnstormers perform in the years after World War I.

The first B-29 landed in the middle of the combat zone, with bomb bay doors frozen open and a fuel supply problem. Missed by Japanese mortar and artillery shells, the plane taxied toward Mount Suribachi. Excited Seabees who'd been building the runway asked the crew whether it was smooth enough.

As soon as the B-29 was repaired, it took off again—Iwo Jima was no place to park, even for a couple of hours. Yet from then on, Marines could look over at the main air-strip and see why they were fighting—if they knew what the scene meant. In those days, privates weren't told the strategic reason for taking Iwo Jima, and, Hudson says, "That probably was a mistake."[97] Still, Marines knew enough: they had an island to take, the Japanese were on it, the Americans needed it, there wasn't a way around it, and it couldn't wait.

Hudson did see planes landing. He remembered hearing about one of them, "The pilot called in and said, 'We have to land,' and they said, 'You can't. The runway's not ready.' They said, 'We're going to land anyway,' and they did."[98] That plane needed a couple days of repairs before it could take off. Another B-29 crew, knowing they wouldn't make it to Tinian, found that half an airstrip was far better than the sea. Aircrew were desperately glad for Iwo Jima, and at least one pilot named his plane for the Marines.

Monday, 5 March 1945

After two straight weeks of battle, 5 March was a rest, a day for reorganizing instead of attacking, though both sides fired mortar and artillery. New men came forward to replace casualties, but, not knowing how to work with the team, often they didn't last long. Replacements were about half as likely as veterans to survive.[99] A combat veteran, now, with a survival record of an entire two weeks, Hudson taught "young and green" replacements how to stay alive.

> I can't remember exactly how many more days we slowly pushed the Japs back, and forced them from their underground tunnels. I just knew that with each day that passed, the men in my squad were fewer and fewer. The Japs hit us hard, but we hit back even harder. Unfortunately, men are killed and it's not easy to forget them.

As the battle went on and on, Hudson tried to train the replacements in his squad, and they managed to fight a little better than their enemies, because their enemy was willing to die, but "we wanted to live."

The rest they got on this day was badly needed, but not nearly sufficient. The noise and stress Marines slept through showed how exhausted they were. "[C]onstant noise: artillery shells, small-arms fire, aircraft noise, just constant. Even the flares made noise when they were shot off."[100]

Sheer exhaustion allowed Hudson to sleep through flares lighting the night sky at least as brightly as daylight. The Marines' nighttime schedule of sleeping one hour at a time may almost have been worse than not sleeping, but few people understood sleep cycles then. Several hours in a foxhole of alternating an hour of sleep with an hour of watching would leave Marines under the impression they were awake and ready for battle in the morning, but in reality, their physical fatigue had been adding up every day, for two weeks so far. Not to mention the mental and emotional fatigue of combat.

> The fatigue and the stress and not knowing what was going to happen next was just too much—and the devastation and the horror. Watching guys next to you get shot and get blown up, and wondering when it's going to be my turn.[101]

Knowledge of how to handle combat was irrelevant to a Marine too exhausted to respond to what was happening. Hudson felt he was overloaded, running on empty, like a train going uphill with no fuel. His idea of paradise became six solid hours of sleep. "I don't remember dreaming. I really don't remember that at all."[102] The interruptions were probably cutting off his sleep before he reached the REM (rapid eye movement) stage. Lack of REM sleep diminishes the ability to think, learn, remember, and perform; not a good set of abilities to lose in combat.

With maybe ten to eleven hours of dark, Hudson should have received four to five hours of sleep, one hour at a time, if things worked out according to plan. "But it never worked out according to the plans if the guy said,

'Hey, you'd better wake up. Something is going on over here.'"[103]

After two weeks, Marines who had landed in top fighting condition could hardly stay awake. What was supposed to be a quick sprint across the island had become a marathon—and, in this battle, even alert men found it hard to stay alive.

Captain Fred Haynes later said,

> Among the frontline veterans, one often saw men who had lost a great deal of weight. Their eye sockets appeared hollow, and there was a strange disjunction between the movement of the head and the eyes. Many very tough Marines were approaching the point where we officers could not expect them to continue fighting indefinitely.[104]

Tuesday, 6 March 1945

The day started with the battle's heaviest artillery barrage: sixty-seven minutes of firing 22,500 shells onto Japanese lines. The Japanese were not impressed; they just increased their return fire.

Artillery was supposed to "soften up" the enemy before attacks, but usually tunnels protected the Japanese. One Japanese trick, since artillery units couldn't see where they were shooting, was to shoot a few of their own shells into Marine front lines when Marine artillery started firing. If Marines on the front lines thought the Japanese shells were friendly fire, they might tell the artillery to stop. But if the smoke color was visible, Marines could tell American shells from Japanese shells.

RCT 25's job for the day was to hold its position on the right. Commanders were concerned about the state of their forces; they could tell the Marines were tired and their leaders inexperienced from their actions, their looks, and missed opportunities. Tired men forgot why they should care about safety, failed to notice threats, and spent too much willpower on just getting up in the morning. Willpower had to last all day, as challenging tasks for a rested man looked impossible to a tired man.

Hudson's platoon lost one of its original Marines in a transfer to the battalion command post. Any such change weakened the platoon. Replacements were like transplanted seedlings, less likely to survive and initially weakly attached.

Wednesday, 7 March 1945

RCT 25 found a Japanese exercise map from January, showing the Japanese had planned for exactly what had happened in the Meat Grinder. The Japanese had also predicted fighting that was yet to come: the Fifth Division's struggle to finish the battle near Kitano Point.

Also on this day, RCT 25 became the only unit building defensive positions (barbed wire, a minefield, cannon, and mortars) while the rest of the Fourth Division drove the Japanese toward them like a hammer to an anvil.

Around this time, Hudson had the chance to shoot a Japanese portable grenade launcher—which his unit called a "knee mortar," since it was knee-shaped. While waiting for the rest of the front line to catch up, the unit found the knee mortar and shells near a cave. The Marines placed barbed wire in front of them so nobody could crawl in and enjoyed the novelty of building a defensive position. For about two days, they stayed in the same place, waiting for everyone else to catch up. They fired the Japanese mortar into Japanese lines. "We didn't know what we were shooting at—no idea that we were aiming at anything. But we knew that we were shooting at someplace else where there were no Marines out in front somewhere."[105]

The Marines were used to being on the receiving end of knee mortars. They knew the Japanese usually fired the three rounds that came in one box as quickly as they could, and rarely fired more than three rounds at a time in the same area. So there was a strategy. "As soon as the first round hit, you took cover and stayed down until the second and third round was fired." Though the knee mortar wasn't a powerful mortar, it could still kill one or two men.

Thursday, 8 March 1945

RCT 25 strengthened its defenses while the rest of the division pushed the Japanese toward RCT 25. Rather than give up, the Japanese managed an organized counterattack that night. For night operations, Japanese assault leaders sometimes wore a strong scent so their men could follow even in complete darkness. Waves of Japanese hit the division after two hours of firing, and there was hand-to-hand fighting all over.

In the blur of days that the battle became, there is one time that stands out in Hudson's memory. Going by surrounding events, this time may have been as early as 26 February or as late as 8 March. Somewhere in there was a night when Hudson's squad got an unexpected break.

Hudson and his men had had little chance to discuss life and death while trying to survive the battle. This night, there was time for conversation, a talk that defined for Hudson what he was fighting for and what he would live for. Hudson learned that night something formal teaching had never taught him: understanding and respect for people and their different lives and personalities.

After a rainy, cold week, Hudson's platoon was rearranged to operate more efficiently. Usually a Marine infantry platoon has four squads of thirteen men; what was left of Hudson's platoon was now combined into two squads of twelve and ten. Martinez promoted Hudson to squad leader, since his squad leader had been shot by a sniper the day before. Hudson was now leading twelve men, and Martinez took the other ten.

Though the majority of the Japanese had been killed during the first week of battle, the Marines had also lost many men. "Our job now," Hudson recalls, "was to rout the Japs from their holes and caves and secure the island so as to make it safe for the air corps to use little Iwo's three great landing strips."

Their first task was to fill a hundred-yard gap between two companies during a banzai attack. At dawn, Hudson checked his men and they started out. They had not moved far when a Nambo machine gun opened up and pinned them down. The first blast didn't hit anyone, but with the second blast two men right behind Hudson were killed. Seeing where the fire came from, the men on the flank put several bazooka shells right in the machine gun nest. The gun stopped and they continued, minus two men. Hudson was now squad leader for ten men.

By the time they reached the next company, they were spread out too far: "when you spread out ten men over one hundred yards with no heavy firepower you aren't in any too good a position." This was one of many times on Iwo Jima when a company didn't have enough men or weapons to cover the rough terrain for its assigned distance. Sometimes it took two understrength companies to cover what one full company could handle on easier terrain.

Hudson reported to the commander of the next company, and they started their morning push together. After getting the signal to move out, Hudson's assistant squad leader Charlie started to go. No sooner had he moved than a sniper bullet shot through his head. Now Hudson was leading nine men and they were pinned down again, spreading out more and more.

Determined that one sniper couldn't hold them down, Hudson got his men moving quickly and staying low, to get to a better position for fighting back. In a few more yards, they came to better terrain. One of the men spotted a mortar crew in a rock formation, and the squad tossed in a few grenades. The grenades scared the Japanese, and they ran one by one across a clearing. The squad shot them one by one. "Morale goes high when you can kill back, and things aren't all one-sided. We felt pretty good and stayed in their rock foundation until we heard more orders of what to do." With nine men in the rock shelter, they were "safe as safe could be," so they waited there for the next move. Contrary to popular opinion shaped by movies, "In combat things go slow and you never know why you have to slow down especially when you are in the mood for moving out and getting the whole mess over with."

While waiting for orders, Hudson had his men dig two foxholes outside the rock formation and put two sentries in each. The rest of the men stayed in the rock formation and tried to catch up on their sleep between taking turns as lookout.

We waited for the Japs to come again that night, and during the hours of darkness when it's cold and you are scared, you talk to your buddies and you seem like brothers to each other, because of the intimacy and warmth of knowing you have a friend who has saved your life and guards you while you sleep in a muddy hole that's not even fit for the land crab that shares it with you.

Outside the rock formation that night, the lines were building up to a solid front, preparing for a bigger push the next day. Inside, Hudson's squad knew that although this was their best chance since the invasion to get some sleep, with dawn bringing their biggest push so far, this was also probably the last night they would be together. None knew who might have hours and who might have decades to live. So they talked, and "each one had something to say that I'll always remember as long as I live."

The statements and the men made an impression lasting over the decades. Other details have faded, such as whether Hudson was leading eight or nine men at this point.. Such details were vital in battle, but not important enough to compete for long-term memory when Hudson was physically, spiritually, and mentally drained.

Hudson's squad, made up of new guys and veterans, older and younger, adventurous and timid, farm and city boys, married and definitely not, reflected the variety found among Marines and among men. Their reactions to the possibility of death also varied widely. Hudson understood fear of death, respecting those who did the job anyway and feeling disdain for the one who didn't. Combat fatigue made some sense to him, but not cowardice. The talk of the men that night, like last words, had special significance for Hudson. He weighed their words against who they were and who they wanted to be.

Yash was a carefree young Polish boy, unfazed by combat. "He just talked about eating a hot meal again and that seemed all he wanted even though he was almost ten thousand miles from home and not sure whether he would ever get there or not." Several days later Yash "cracked up and cried like a baby" after seeing another Marine lose his arm.

Carlton was married, with a baby girl. He wanted to go home and quit digging foxholes in hard volcanic rock. He swore he wouldn't dig in again, and in fact the next day a mortar landed near him and put a fist-sized piece of shell through his shoulder. "He smiled when he was hit and said, 'I'm going back to my daughter now.'"

Red was much older, in his thirties, a new man in the squad. Hudson thought "the infantry was no place for him. He never said much because he was too afraid." Yet Hudson called him a good Marine and said he killed over fifteen Japanese in one night raid. Several days later he was killed by a sniper. "The odds sort of go against a man."

Saint's nickname came from having a French name, not being a saint. Hudson called him the comedian in the squad, but even the comedian cried when things got tough. On this night he was happy, and talked about his first love affair with a gorgeous blonde back in California. He wasn't very concerned with the seriousness of fighting; he just wanted to go back and have more love affairs. The shell that hit Carlton also hit Saint—in his abdomen. The squad thought he would die, but, while being carried away on the stretcher, he was able to wave goodbye.

Irish had only been in the Corps for a year. He missed Staten Island more than anything else in the world. He fought hard, one night killing a Japanese soldier with a knife. His hope was to get home and marry his sweetheart, but several days later, a shell landed in his foxhole. "We all thought he would be all right even though his legs were badly injured, but he died on the hospital ship several days later."

Another man, who will remain nameless for obvious reasons, "was a coward and everyone knew it. Perhaps you can't condemn a man when he isn't sure of living or dying, but he was a disgrace to the Marine Corps and everything we believed in." He lived through the battle by developing a toothache before the big push the next day. He went back to the aid station and stayed until the battle was over.

Whit, from Massachusetts, "was a corporal and a good one too." He talked about going home, being satisfied, and never complaining about anything anymore. "He thought that just living was wonderful and to be able to sleep just eight hours would be heaven. He got his wish— Whit and I still correspond and I know he sure does appreciate living now."

John, a big strong man who thrived on adventure, "wanted to get off this rock island and fast." He told the others what he planned to do in Honolulu with his back pay and a five-day leave after the battle was over. He had lost a brother in France several weeks before and knew he would need to take care of his parents when he got back home to the farm. But he was not able to. "Johnny picked up three machine gun bullets in the chest the very next morning and died in my arms, cursing the Japs for what they did to him."

Against a background of filth, dirt, and horror shone brotherly love, life lessons, and understanding of what it means to be American. Both the good and the bad were beyond expressing, but Hudson tried:

I haven't the verbal ability to describe all the fight and horror of war I saw on Iwo Jima. I haven't the power of expression to make you realize the filth and dirt of living in a hole for a month. And perhaps I am failing in telling you of the story of my group, my men, who trusted in me to lead them in combat, of whom many were killed and many will never be the same because of what happened to them. But I did learn a lesson, a lesson so strong and lasting that it changed my whole way of life. I've recovered from my wounds, and overcome all the mental strain that war caused, but it was this group of loyal men who made me realize everything I was fighting for, they gave me the ability to see other persons' worlds through that person's own background and experience and sense of values, to respect the rights of others, to help a person when he needs help, and everything that adds up to the American way of life.

Friday, 9 March 1945

This was the day Turkey Knob finally fell, as RCT 25 stormed Japanese positions which had held out nearly two weeks. In some places, RCT 25 advanced several hundred yards—an exceptional distance—joining another regiment and leaving only scattered pockets of resistance behind. The Third Division, crossing the center of the island, split Japanese forces in two by reaching the sea, and sent back a canteen of seawater (for inspecting, not drinking, they explained) to prove their accomplishment.

The right flank, where the 3/25 battalion was, had moved less than one thousand yards in two weeks; it was the door hinge the rest of the Fourth Division swung around.

The man Hudson already knew as "a coward—and a disgrace to the Marine Corps" left the platoon because of a toothache.

Saturday, 10 March 1945

The last part of the battle began. Marines found and sealed Japanese caves one by one with explosives and bull-dozers. Resistance was dying out, and more units reached the ocean. RCT 25, however, was in for five more days of fierce battle. What RCT 25 faced was the last stand of the Japanese on the eastern side of the island.

The Japanese stayed in their tunnels during American artillery fire. Afterward, they would come out firing with

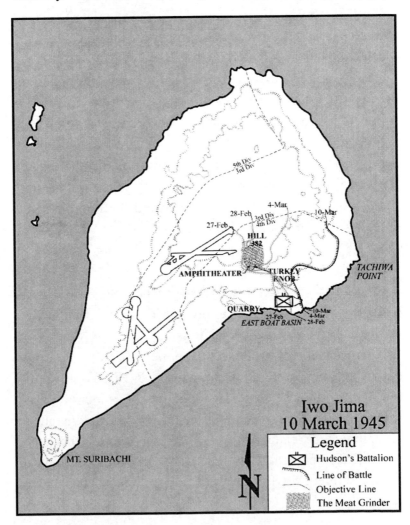

Iwo Jima
10 March 1945

Legend

⊠ Hudson's Battalion
Line of Battle
Objective Line
The Meat Grinder

everything they had while the Marines advanced. When Marine casualties rose to the point that the advance stopped, the Japanese would return to the tunnels and come out elsewhere to do the same thing.

One Marine in Hudson's platoon was hit by a sniper and another by a US Navy shell. Very few of the original men were left; almost everyone was a replacement.

Sunday, 11 March 1945

RCT 25 was hit by heavy fire from the deep crevices and ridges, in bitter fighting throughout the day, and one Marine in Hudson's platoon was killed by a sniper.

A captured Japanese soldier said there were hundreds of Japanese with weapons and water but little food in the small area ahead of the division. Also, there was a Japanese major general. Probably, the division was facing General Senda, commander of the major army unit on the island. The terrain in the area was rough rocky outcroppings and such scrubby vegetation as had survived the bombing; the defenders had excellent cover.

Monday, 12 March 1945

Eight days after the first B-29 landing, Iwo Jima's main airstrip was so much improved it was handling heavy traffic, not just emergency landings.

Northeast of that airstrip, General Cates, the commander of the Fourth Division, paused RCT 25's attack on the pocket thought to be Senda's final headquarters and tried to reach Senda by loudspeaker. In his statement, he complimented Senda on his heroic fight, warned that there was no further benefit in resistance or death, guaranteed good treatment for the staff as well as Senda, and assured him that he could honorably surrender, living to serve Japan in the future.

If Senda considered the source, the statement was highly complimentary. Cates understood heroic fighting. As a lieutenant at Belleau Wood in World War I, Cates had become famous for reporting that with most of his men gone, lacking support, and under constant fire, he would hold. Senda's thoughts, however, cannot be known; the loudspeaker malfunctioned, and whether or not the Japanese heard, they kept shooting. After two hours, one casualty, and some damage, the Marines restarted the attack.

Tuesday, 13 March 1945

RCT 25 devoted another day to the fight to finish off the pocket of resistance.

At some point in the battle, the platoon had a new lieutenant assigned as their platoon leader. Most likely a recent graduate of a 90-day officer training course (called "90-day wonders" behind their backs), like many lieutenants, this one had more information but less experience than the men he led. Hudson remembered him once "lying down and yelling at us to, 'Move out, move out.' He didn't know what . . . he was talking about. See, I got salty. I was an experienced combat veteran."[106] Hudson and the others had already moved out, following Martinez, and were surveying the situation. The lieutenant should have been leading them instead of lying down behind them.

"Marty was the one that told us what to do."[107] On paper the platoon followed an officer, but in practice, the platoon followed experience, not rank. Martinez, still unwounded, continued to act as the platoon leader. Back in February, Hudson had been as new to combat as the lieutenant. But that was a long time ago—weeks had passed.

Now he and the other combat veterans of the platoon tolerated their new officer and taught him how to function.

Wednesday, 14 March 1945

The official flag was raised at headquarters, declaring the battle over. The Fourth Division started shipping out. These events seemed to have nothing to do with RCT 25, which was still fighting the pocket.

In Hudson's platoon, another Marine got hit. Besides the men already mentioned, the platoon had lost other original members, including one taken out for combat fatigue, one who lost an eye, one who lost his legs, one who was transferred to the company command post, and one who went missing for twenty days but later rejoined the outfit, ending up at the company command post. Replacements arrived and tried to fill the gaps, but the core of the platoon continued to be the few men who remained from the invasion, the ones who knew what to do and how to do it.

Hudson was not impressed by generals deciding the main part of the fighting was over and declaring the island secure. "It was down there, maybe, but not where we were. We still were wiping out caves and tunnels, doing what we did through the whole thing. And there were still many of them still alive and fighting."[108]

The commanders, however, needed excuses to declare the battle over, to reassure war-weary Americans back home who didn't know what the Marines were up against. Three Marine divisions, fighting for weeks, hadn't taken an island too small to find on a world map?

5

Lying Next to a Bundle of Explosion

*Bill was wounded when he exchanged grenades
with a Jap. Dare to say the Jap lost that toss.*
— Sgt Manuel Martinez, 3-K-25, Fourth Division[109]

Thursday, 15 March 1945

Only two of the original forty-seven men in Hudson's platoon were present at the end of the battle. Hudson wasn't one of them. The platoon was near Tachiwa Point on the last day of the Fourth Division's battle; the ocean was only a short sprint away. It was while finishing off the last Japanese strong point in the Fourth Division's zone that Private First Class William Hudson was wounded by grenade shrapnel. He became his unit's last casualty. "Pretty lucky," Hudson said, maybe even "dumb."[110]

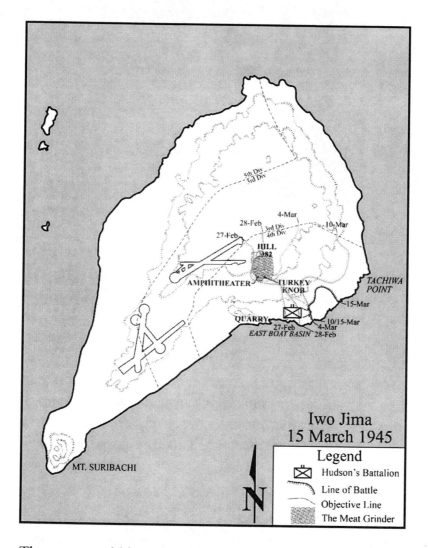

Iwo Jima
15 March 1945

Legend

Hudson's Battalion
Line of Battle
Objective Line
The Meat Grinder

They were within a hundred yards of the ocean when it happened; they could see the water, and Martinez told them their battle would be over when they got to the ocean. He challenged them to get down there and get it over with.

Hudson saw a gun emplacement firing off to his right, saw a machine gun kill four men, and realized from where he was, he could see into the back part of the emplacement. "I said, 'I can get in there and throw a grenade in there without them seeing me.' I don't know why I did it; I was pretty dumb, I guess."[111]

Laying down his BAR, he took two grenades, sneaked up behind the emplacement, and threw in a grenade. A Japanese soldier came out of the hole, looked at Hudson, and threw a grenade at him. Hudson ducked into a slight depression, and the Japanese grenade landed a few feet from his head. "I heard the grenade I had thrown go off and I knew that I put the machine gun out of commission. But I also knew that I was lying next to a bundle of explosion, but I was too amazed to move."

American and Japanese grenades were different, and the differences probably saved Hudson's life. American grenades had a pin to pull; the Marine would throw the grenade and hope it went far enough away. The Japanese grenade was detonated by hitting the firing pin on a hard object, often the soldier's helmet. "When we heard a distinct clank, we knew a grenade would be thrown and we quickly took cover." The Japanese grenade was less powerful and had more explosive than shrapnel; its effect was more of a concussive blow.

Hudson sat and counted the seconds until the Japanese grenade went off. When it exploded, the blast went mostly above him. Shrapnel hit him in the wrist, upper arm, and the back of his neck. But he didn't know yet that he was wounded.

The concussion and the noise got me kind of goofy. I couldn't hear, but I wasn't aware of that either. I had one more grenade, and I got up, and I threw the other grenade in this bunker. I backed off, and that went off, and I knew that anybody that was in there was probably dead.[112]

The Battle of Iwo Jima was over for PFC William Hudson. "At that time a corpsman came up to me, and I knew I was wounded. But I wasn't in any pain, because I was in shock. I don't know if he said anything to me; I don't remember."[113]

The corpsman bandaged Hudson's arm and wrist and wrapped a bandage around his neck "because I had a little scrape on the back of my neck."[114] The corpsman told Hudson he'd be going back to the field hospital and put Hudson on a jeep that was already carrying another wounded Marine. Despite morphine and shock, Hudson was now in a lot of pain.

> I was going to tell the corpsman how much I hurt, but there was another Marine on the jeep who had a severe abdominal wound. He was moaning in pain, and after I saw how badly he was hit, I didn't say another word.

By this point in the battle, those hurt badly enough to need a real hospital could be evacuated by air. But on his arrival at the field hospital, Hudson was able to walk in. Another corpsman put a new dressing on his wounds and told him they would leave the shrapnel in for now since it didn't look that bad. Then he told Hudson to lie down on a cot and get some sleep.

> So I hit that cot, and . . . I fell asleep. That was the most peaceful, happy sleep I had in a month. I felt relieved, and I knew I was alive. I knew I was wounded, but I didn't know to what extent I was wounded. I couldn't talk. My tongue and my teeth seemed like they were loose, and I couldn't hear too

well because of the concussion. But I thought I was okay.[115]

That night, about sixty Japanese tried an escape from the pocket Hudson had been fighting, and failed. Failure seemed to break their spirit. Across much of the island, more Japanese were behind American lines than in front, so at night Marines still shot first and asked questions later.

When Hudson woke up, he was lying on his back. He started trying to figure out how bad the damage was.

I couldn't move the left arm because of the shot. I had been a gymnast in school also, and my first thought was, "All my training gone to waste." . . . I didn't think I could use my hands and arms anymore. . . . I didn't think I was paralyzed, but I thought I was wounded and couldn't use my arms. But then I started moving my fingers, and I said, "That's not bad." And I could move my arms. Then I felt fine.[116]

Since the time the Marines set sail for Iwo Jima, Hudson's parents hadn't heard from their son. In some ways, no news was good news; if he was wounded or killed, they would be notified—though not necessarily soon. Finally, Hudson's parents got a letter from U.S. Marine Corps Headquarters saying their son received "shrapnel wounds of the arm and neck in action against the enemy on 15 March, 1945 at Iwo Jima, Volcano Islands." They didn't get much information, just enough to raise both hopes and fears. But the news was better than other families were getting from Iwo Jima.

Hudson sent his own letter the day he was wounded, saying:

I know you will be anxious to hear from me because of the little session we are going through here. First of all I want to say that I am feeling fine and everything will be all right from now on.

Don't be worried when I say that I am at a field hospital now. I got a few pieces of shrapnel in my arm and hand but it isn't serious at all.

Our outfit was on the line since D-Day and I got through OK until this A.M. when I was hit by a grenade. Please don't worry about me because things are going along well here. I will write again as soon as possible so until then it will be soon. All my love to all. Your loving son, Bill

P.S. God was with me I know.

Friday, 16 March 1945

Hudson's Japanese flag, the one he'd held up as a battle souvenir in the picture taken of him during the battle, got stolen while he was at the field hospital.

One of the amphibious vehicles took Hudson out to a ship to go back to Pearl Harbor. On board ship, Hudson got a shower, even with all his bandages on. A corpsman took his dressings off, "patched me up again,"[117] and showed Hudson to a bed. "I got in a bed with sheets. That was a luxury that most people never feel grateful for, to think of the simple fact of getting in a bed with sheets and a blanket and nobody shooting at you."[118]

Hudson wrote a letter sparkling with joy at being alive.

At the present time I guess I am just about the happiest marine here—the battle for little Iwo is all over for me and I am safe and sound now; to add to my great happiness I just completed a shower and shave and hot chow for the first time in 26 days. Now I am lying in a sack with a mattress and sheets and pillow and all the trimmings. We even have a radio playing and the music just fits in perfect.

I will be able to write every day now so I hope it makes up for the great interlapse since my last letter. Although I will be able to write daily I don't know when my letters will be mailed. Well regardless of that I'm going to write anyway so you will get a big stack of mail just like I will get soon.

While on the island I did receive some mail and I have it all in my gas mask now. I can't get at it now but I will try to answer everything you asked. I think the latest letter I received was dated the 23rd of Feb.

I know you will continue to worry about why, when and how I was wounded. I want to say that your worries are all over because I am really fine and the few pieces of shrapnel I have won't even show a scar when they heal up and they are well on the way now, and by the time we get back to the rest camp I will be back with my boys again in good shape, raring to go through some more training etc.

The P.S. said,

I am so happy and thankful for everything now I can't express my feelings.

In the morning, there was some fight left in the pocket of Japanese, but Japanese organization had fallen apart and resistance quickly ended. By midmorning, all Marine battalions reached the beach road. The pocket was taken.

Hudson's platoon stayed on Iwo Jima a couple more days before returning to Hawaii, but its fight was over. Of the original Marines of Hudson's platoon, only Whit and Martinez finished the battle with the platoon. Martinez eventually received the Silver Star.

Iwo Jima was declared secured that evening, meaning organized resistance was supposed to be over. For the Fourth Division that was true. The Fifth Division, on the north end of the island, had ten days of heavy combat to go.

Saturday, 17 March 1945

Admiral Nimitz memorably announced in his Communique to the Pacific Fleet, "Among the Americans who served on Iwo Island uncommon valor was a common virtue,"[119] even as battle continued on the other side of the island.

Monday, 19 March 1945

The Fourth Division's last units boarded ship. They sailed for Maui, Hawaii the next day.

Eventually, the mail sent during the battle caught up with Hudson, and he got to read his letters, Valentine's Day cards, and St. Patrick's Day cards all at once. He wrote back, "I didn't even realize that Valentine's day was here or over and St. Patrick's day didn't even come in my mind at all. I guess we were a little bit too busy for things like that on Iwo. . . ."

6

Show a Burning Determination

Monday, 26 March 1945

Five weeks before, the first US troops had cut their way across the island, but that hadn't ended the battle. The battle wasn't over on 23 February, when Marines raised the flag on Mt. Suribachi; nor on 4 March, when the first B-29 landed on the island; nor on 9 March, when the backbone of the Japanese defense broke; nor on 14 March, at the official flag-raising at headquarters; nor on 16 March, when the Fourth Division reached the sea; nor on 17 March, when Admiral Nimitz congratulated the Marines on their victory; nor on 25 March, when the Fifth Division pushed through the last Japanese holdouts to the sea at the northwest corner of the island.

The Japanese attacked for the last time on 26 March in a well-laid plan to create maximum confusion and destruction. In the early morning hours, two hundred fifty Japanese and fifty-three Americans died as Japanese soldiers attacked pilots sleeping near the airfield. One could say the end of the battle came later on 26 March, when the island was declared secure. Or maybe the battle ended several years later, when the last Japanese soldier came out of hiding and surrendered.

Seventy years later, it is probably safe today to say that nobody is still fighting the Battle of Iwo Jima.

The Battle of Iwo Jima stretched over at least thirty-six days.[120] Most battles end in minutes or hours. Iwo Jima cost 21,865 US casualties who survived and 6,821 killed.[121] (Casualties, often confused with those killed in battle, are the total of soldiers no longer able to continue fighting, because they are dead, wounded, prisoners, shell-shocked, missing, or even deserters. Usually the majority of casualties are the wounded, and those killed are a much smaller fraction. The point in counting casualties is not what happened to them, but how many aren't available for the next battle.) More than nine in ten Japanese defenders died on the island[122] rather than surrender.

There's never been a battle like Iwo Jima in the history of the US Marine Corps; Iwo Jima ranks among the greatest battles in the history of mankind. More than fifteen thousand men per square mile[123] fought over Iwo Jima. About a fifth of them, or three thousand men per square mile,[124] died there.[125] Ongoing battle meant artillery fire was normal background noise, and artillery flares at night gave enough light to read by. There was no safe place, nowhere to relax. Even behind the lines, Japanese would pop up from underground and shoot, giving the battle the name, "Prairie Dog War."

One Iwo Jima veteran was surveyed in 1995 by the Marine Corps' History Division about whether his training was adequate for combat. "Yes," he answered. "But I am not sure that any training could prepare you for Iwo."[126]

Americans greatly outnumbered Japanese—this was war, not a fair fight. The saying among soldiers is: if you're in a fair fight, you didn't plan it well enough. But the Japanese defenses and their will to fight mattered more than numbers. Almost no Japanese surrendered during the battle; Marines captured only 1% of the Japanese force.[127] When the Marines left, as much as 10%[128] of the Japanese force remained alive, hidden, and mostly still fighting. About eight hundred of these would later be killed. In the end, about 92% of the Japanese on the island died there, whether at their own hands or at those of the Marines.[129] When the Marines left, weeks later than scheduled, thinking maybe three hundred Japanese soldiers remained hidden in caves for the Army and Navy to deal with, there were several times that many.

Finding over 22,000 Japanese hiding in caves and tunnels cost almost 29,000 American wounded or dead. In other words, for every three dead Japanese, three Americans were seriously wounded and another American died.[*] The casualty rate of some infantry regiments reached 75%, leaving very few Marines who fought the battle from start to finish. There were very few Japanese left at all.

Marines remember Iwo Jima, their bloodiest and hardest battle, as proof that Marines work together, keep

---

[*] Japanese numbers are vague, since those who might have known exact numbers were themselves dead. Specific numbers for American deaths depend on whether to include the missing, those who died later of battle wounds, or all Americans or just Marines. Haynes and Warren, *Lions of Iwo Jima*, 8, gives 22,000 defenders, 28,000 American casualties, and fewer than 2000 Japanese who survived. Buell, *Uncommon Valor, Common Virtue*, 219, says total American casualties were 28,868, of whom 6821 died.

on, and finish the job no matter what. They expected victory even if it was the last surviving Marine who won, and sometimes it looked as if victory would cost exactly that, as General Erskine observed while dedicating a cemetery on the island. Victory cost so much because the Japanese expected to spend the life of every soldier, preferring death to surrender, insisting on victory or annihilation, and discussing peace only on their own terms. They refused to be taken prisoner and despised the prisoners they took. But the Marines were also determined; most Marines had joined intending to do at least their share of saving the world.[130]

This was not a battle of big troop movements; the man, the squad, and the platoon fought the battle. Where heavy armament couldn't move forward, human flesh won. Major General Fred Haynes, a captain at Iwo Jima, said the battle pitted Marine flesh against Japanese concrete.[131]

The Fourth Division, with Bill Hudson, moved less than a hundred yards some days. Over twenty-six days, the division landed on the right side of the beach, headed north, and later swung around east, to finish on the northeast part of the island. Hudson's unit traveled a mile or two during this time, moving on average ten or fifteen feet per hour. A snail could have crossed Iwo Jima with them.

Almost half of the Fourth Division, 9,098 men, became casualties, of whom 1,806 were killed in action. The division counted 8,982 Japanese killed in its zone, with another thousand believed buried. The Fourth took only forty-four prisoners.

The Fifth Division landed on the left side of the beach, and four days later that division took Mount Suribachi. The Fifth took thirty-six total days to swing around the far side of the island to the northwest point, in combat all the way.

The Third Division was held in reserve for a few days until the Fourth and Fifth Divisions were so beaten up that the support of a fresh division was needed. The Third then went up the middle of the island between the other two.

"Talk to any veteran of Iwo Jima," said the Marine Corps Director of History and Museums, Colonel John W. Ripley, quoted in Larry Smith's book *Iwo Jima: World War II Veterans Remember the Greatest Battle of the Pacific*, "and he's going to tell you . . . we had it far worse than anyone else. And you know what? Every single one of these guys is right. Their fight was tough. There wasn't any such thing as an easy run on Iwo Jima."[132]

Of the total force of the Third, Fourth, and Fifth Divisions, about one in three men became a casualty, and about one in ten was killed.[133] One third of all Marine losses in World War II resulted from Iwo Jima. About one third of World War II Medals of Honor were awarded for Iwo Jima. More Americans died per month at Iwo Jima than in the average year in Vietnam.

Yet Iwo Jima would still be unknown if the airplane had been invented twenty years earlier or later.[*] During and after the battle, the Seabees worked furiously, moving three million cubic yards of volcanic earth, preparing the airfields and building the longest runway in the Pacific. At the time, Hudson's reason for fighting for the island was that he had been told to do so. After learning more later, he

---

[*] Long-distance air travel quickly became regular and reliable in the years after WWII; for the 707 airframe or the DC-3, Iwo Jima would have been nice but unnecessary. But 20 years before 1945, in the era of Lindbergh's flight, Iwo Jima would have been useless. Lindbergh had to strip an airplane to gas tank and wings to get from New York to Paris—a standard airplane with a standard load couldn't have even flown from Iwo Jima to Tokyo and back.

came to his own conclusions on whether the battle was worth the cost.

> We got it, and we got those airfields in shape, and our B-29s could make emergency landings on there. We could put some of our Air Force fighters on there. We destroyed the Japanese communications so they couldn't radio back to Japan that the B-29s were coming. So I guess 6,841 dead Marines was worth maybe saving 10,000 airmen, whose lives were saved because they could make emergency landings on Iwo Jima.[134]

Before battle ended on Iwo Jima, thirty-five B-29s, with their crews of over 350, had already used the airstrips. Iwo Jima actually held three airfields: one near the landing beach, one near the Meat Grinder, and one the Japanese had been building northeast of the other two. The airfields grew quickly after the battle, and the Seabees and Army kept lengthening and building runways through the end of the war. By the end of the war a few months later, 2,251 B-29s, with crews totaling 24,761, had landed, and Iwo Jima was launching both fighter escorts and air-sea rescues. Fighters were actually the original reason to take the island—to create a fighter base close enough to attack Japan. But late in the war, firebombing Japan became the main strategy, so Iwo Jima's main job turned into bomber support.

The Air Corps had been bombing Japan for some time. The bombs caused some destruction, but many B-29s were lost, and the Japanese weren't convinced to shorten the war. So, about the time battle began on Iwo Jima, the Air Corps switched to massive B-29 firebombing raids, launched from the Mariana Islands, dropping jellied gasoline and magnesium on the wood-and-paper structures of Japan. Jellied gasoline, also called napalm and used in flamethrowers on Iwo Jima, is an ancient weapon, similar to the Greek fire used by the Byzantines. Magnesium combined with the gasoline is deadly. As a good heat conductor, magnesium is hard to light on fire. Once lit, however, it is very hard to put out, burning with such a hot flame that it can burn in water.

Where quick-built structures clustered in Japan's industrial areas, one firebomb could do great damage. A few days before Hudson was wounded, 334 B-29s[135] with firebombs did more damage than either atomic bomb. In fact, this attack was the most destructive single bombing mission of the war, but the firebombing didn't shock people the way the atomic bombs did. One expects damage from 334 planeloads of *anything*.

Sun Tzu recommended dry weather and a rising wind for attacks with fire.[136] Tokyo was very windy in the early morning of 10 March 1945. The flames the firebombs started reached hundreds of feet into the air. Fire winds rushed up and down the streets. Some people survived inside non-flammable buildings, if they could breathe as the fire sucked out oxygen. A Japanese newspaperman described the city as being sunrise-bright; he feared all of Tokyo was burned to ashes. Close to 84,000 people were killed, 41,000 wounded, and a million left homeless.

Of the 334 B-29s that delivered the fire, fourteen were lost at sea and five of their crews rescued. Two landed on Iwo Jima while battle continued nearby.

More fire followed. Over ten days, an area averaging the size of Iwo Jima was flattened in each of Tokyo, Nagoya, Kobe, and Osaka, Japan's four most important centers—thirty-two square miles total.

Firebombing must have been a great shock to Japan. Attack from above was still a new idea, and World War II's senior officers were older than powered flight.[137] World War I introduced the idea of attacking an enemy's homeland hundreds of miles behind front lines, but this was the first war to use bombing strategically.

The firebombing brought the war to Japan, showing the Japanese what they had unleashed on the Pacific. The United States hoped to break, or at least weaken, the incredible Japanese will to fight before the time came to invade Japan itself.

Shocked or not, Japan's will to fight remained unbroken—though Japan's people were stunned at losing Iwo Jima, the first piece of Japanese homeland; the first break in the inner defensive ring around the home islands. The loss told the Imperial Japanese Army they could not succeed in pushing back American invasion from the sea. Japan could fight, but it could not win.

Certain defeat was no reason to quit. Japan's premier announced the loss of Iwo Jima by radio, telling listeners to show "a burning determination" to defend Japan. He told them there would be no unconditional surrender; the last living Japanese must fight until the enemy's ambitions were shattered.

For civilians as well as soldiers, loyal sacrifice was a way of life. A Japanese soldier's wife wrote him of her plans to take up his sword when the enemy came and, along with their children, die attacking the enemy.

Even after Iwo Jima was officially lost, the Japanese left there kept fighting. Many expected to win as soon as help arrived. Eventually, they gave up hope, and many walked into US areas on their own, but the last two did not surrender for four years. General Kuribayashi probably died in March, but nobody knows for certain what happened to him. He may have died in a last stand, or he may have killed himself in the officers' ritual suicide, with his aides beheading him afterward. In 1968, the Japanese excavated the general's headquarters cave, which went four stories deep. They found the food and water were mostly gone, but that Kuribayashi still had had communication, medical supplies, and ammunition. The area was untouched by bombing.

The excavation also discovered a hospital cave, with more than 40 Japanese wounded soldiers. Someone had given each one a grenade and told them the time had come. They had all committed suicide rather than surrender.

Wounded Marines like Hudson were helped to live rather than to die. A doctor at a Pearl Harbor hospital said Hudson's shrapnel would be better left in than taken out. Shrapnel, which is hot when it hits, cauterizes wounds, so infection is not a great danger. But shrapnel can move around in the body, causing problems later. Eventually, a piece in Hudson's wrist had to be removed. He still has a piece of shrapnel in his upper arm.

World War II did not wind down slowly; the worst combat of the war was in its last few months. After a year and a half in the Marines, Hudson finally had seen a month of action. He decided it was "more than anybody needed to see in a lifetime." While recovering, Hudson had plenty of time to think about the battle and all the men in his platoon who didn't survive. "I knew things were rough, but I didn't realize how bad things were until I made a list of the men in my platoon and what happened to them."

Though Hudson today would rather not have to remember the battle itself, the men he fought with were "a group of men I'll always remember." Looking back over a lifetime of meeting all kinds of people, from the perspective of decades, Hudson's conclusion is,

> In my whole life I never had the experience of being with a group of men who were so close, so devoted, so dependable, so brave, and so afraid. For twenty-six days I fought with these men, saw them kill, die, laugh, cry, pray, scream, and go stark mad.

Hudson's list of his platoon, made while recovering from wounds, concussion, and lack of sleep, doesn't completely match a list written for another purpose many years later, when there had been time for rumors to be confirmed or denied by records. Like the timing of events during the battle, descriptions in this book of what happened when and to whom are only best guesses from combining several accounts.

Lack of certainty should be no surprise; what is surprising is that anyone knows anything after a battle—when both sides are trying to deceive each other, when the soldiers closest to the events have no time to think, and when the men experiencing the events are the most likely to be dead or incapacitated. Besides, in many cases, a complete understanding of the situation is deliberately hidden from common soldiers, to keep them from the demoralization that could lose a battle. Since ancient times, generals have been advised to tell soldiers good news but keep quiet about bad news.[138]

Despite this, soldiers can and do make good guesses from what they've seen. Hudson began realizing how formidable his enemy had been . . . and how many of them were left in Japan.

7

Kublai Khan Failed to Invade Japan

April 1945

The Fourth Division was welcomed back to Maui with alohas. Now there was time to rest, recover, and count how many rifles, shoes, uniforms, and men were needed to bring the division back to full strength. It was time to get back to shaving, bathing, and using proper military protocol.

In a unit returning from combat, military protocol is more easily ordered than achieved, as reflected in the old saying: no combat-ready unit has ever passed inspection, and no inspection-ready unit has ever passed combat. Hudson's lieutenant told the platoon to stop using his nickname and call him by his title. The proper answer was, "Yes, sir!"

The actual answer was "Okay," with his nickname. "He didn't like that at all," Hudson remembers. "He just thought, 'You guys are not treating me right.'"[139]

Hudson's letters got more serious as he recovered. In early April, he answered questions from his family, who were naturally curious what battle was like, and had asked how many Japanese he had killed. He warned them they might not like what he had to say. Decades later, when he published his letters, knowing he was addressing a more critical generation, he also warned his audience not to take lightly the sacrifice of those who fought:

> While you read [the letters], try to put yourself in a position to think about what it was like during World War II. I knew that the Japs were the enemy and my mission was to destroy them. The Japs were ferocious soldiers who fought with total disregard for life. I was trained to kill or be killed. I was proud of what I did on Iwo Jima, and proud that I served with a group of very brave men. I trained and lived with these men, and our lives were dependent on each other. I still grieve for those who were killed, even though this event happened over half a century ago. Many times I think of these heroes who gave up their future so that you and I could have one.

So, at the age of nineteen, Hudson described what he had lately lived through.

> I don't like to write things about it but in all your letters you did seem very interested in all the scoop. So if you can take it here goes. I doubt if I

could ever describe my feelings all the while I was on the island—I've seen some pretty gruesome things, sights that I'll never be able to get out of my mind as long as I live. I saw some of my best buddies killed and blown to bits, it isn't easy to take but there isn't very much you can do about it but keep fighting on and kill all and as many Japs as you can. I killed my first Jap [on the third day] and then 2 minutes after that I got another. It was good for my morale, to put those Japs out of business. I actually felt good, perhaps I got the lust to kill after that and I was eager to kill as many as I could. The Japs don't fight like we do in the day time they dig in and snipe at you and you can't see a thing—they wait till it's dark and then they start running around playing hand grenade, hand grenade, who gets the shrapnel. They usually get it at night because we are dug in and just wait for them to come. The only thing wrong is that they come from all over, under and every way into your lines, there were so many caves and tunnels over there. I doubt very much if they are all dead, they are probably still running around loose. We usually sleep an hour and watch an hour and no matter how much noise is going on you can always sleep when it's your turn because you are so tired. We had a field day one night and next A.M. there were over 200 Japs in front of our lines—I shot off about 15 magazines of BAR ammo. It's 20 rounds to a magazine. I guess I'll never know how many I did get then. But I had a hot time.

During the whole battle our outfit was on the front all but 5 days—that's when we got some mail and it was good to hear from you. When you're in reserve you clean your weapon and rest, you need both very badly. When we move out we blow up caves and pillboxes by the hundreds and you never know how many Japs you really get by yourself.

I don't know how many Japs I killed all together but for the final question I got plenty, there were lots there and the island was so small everyone got their share.

I remember Dad telling us about the last war—he sure did see action (from the ship) that's good duty. But this way is not so hot. I didn't get a hot meal in 25 days, no shave or shower, no change of clothes except socks. Those K rations get mighty sad after a week or so.

Hudson appreciated the hot meals he now had, and the mail from home, but he was glad for one thing above all. "The best thing about it is the fact that there are no wild Japs running around and no bang bang all day and night."

Another tremendous battle followed Iwo Jima from early April to mid-June: Okinawa, 350 miles from Japan, with good harbors and room to prepare troops for invading Japan. Before Iwo Jima, plans were for the Third, Fourth, and Fifth Divisions to attack Okinawa. Instead, the Marines had to use two completely different divisions while the Third, Fourth, and Fifth recovered.

Okinawa cost over 12,500 Americans killed or missing, and 110,000 Japanese,[140] making the battle the bloodiest one the US experienced in the Pacific War. A tenth to a third of the civilians also died, partly from more Japanese-led mass suicides, and partly because it was hard to tell who was a civilian.

In early April, the Soviet Union warned the Japanese embassy that the Soviet Union was no longer neutral, although it had not yet formally declared war. The announcement coming from Japan's gigantic neighbor was one more unsettling development for Japan to consider. That same week, General MacArthur and Admiral Nimitz got orders to prepare for the war's final stage: Operation Olympic, the invasion of Japan. It was scheduled for November.

Japan prepared for the invasion too. Tsunezo Wachi, the garrison commander of Iwo Jima in 1944, had attacked "with the utmost zeal"[141] the B-29s coming from Saipan. Authorities ordered Wachi to leave Iwo Jima a few months before the battle, and Wachi prepared for the invasion of Japan with equal zeal, training sixteen- and seventeen-year-old volunteers to attack enemy submarines using suicide torpedo boats with a one-way fuel load. He found the young attackers were too wild; they had to be taught the discipline of waiting for the most effective moment to die for their country.

In March, all men ages fifteen to sixty and all women seventeen to forty had been drafted into a Patriotic Citizens Fighting Corps. There was no money for weapons or uniforms, so they prepared with what was available. A high-school girl was given an awl and told to aim at the enemy's abdomen. Facing this non-uniformed force, American troops would have to either kill everyone or risk their lives guessing who was a civilian. Taking Iwo Jima over the dead bodies of nine out of ten of its defenders had been hard. Were Americans prepared to kill nine out of ten Japanese mothers and teenage daughters in their homes?

Japanese leaders bet American morale would break first. Betting wrong meant Japan would be extinct. Betting right meant Japan could continue the fight, or at least surrender on better terms. Yet how could Japan surrender the

Medals

The **Medal of Honor** that Chambers received is the highest military decoration for valor, presented by the President. Military members receive the medal for conspicuous gallantry and intrepidity at the risk of life above and beyond the call of duty while in action against an enemy. Such a risk of life means many recipients of the Medal of Honor don't live to receive the honor.

A Medal of Honor wearer is saluted by all ranks of the military before anyone else is saluted. Calling someone a "winner" of this medal is incorrect, because there isn't a competition. Those who receive the medal are "recipients" or "awardees." There were only 464 recipients of the Medal of Honor in World War II, out of more than sixteen million Americans.

The **Silver Star** that Martinez received is the third-highest military decoration (after the Navy Cross and the Medal of Honor) he could have received. The award is for gallantry while in action against an enemy, beyond the level of any lower combat decoration but not at the level of the Navy Cross.

The **Bronze Star Medal** that Hudson received is the fourth-highest combat award (ninth-highest military award), given for bravery, heroism, or meritorious service. The Bronze Star Medal is not the same as the bronze service star that is given just for participating in a battle.

The **Purple Heart Medal**, which was not needed for the invasion of Japan, is given to military members wounded or killed by the enemy.

homeland at all? Japan could not disgrace the emperor and the emperor's ancestors. Japan could not forget the sacrifice of Japanese soldiers, who had written on every battlefield in their own blood that there would be no surrender— and the closer to Japan, the harder the fight.[142]

President Roosevelt died on 12 April 1945, and his almost unknown vice president Harry Truman was inaugurated as President. On the same day, Hudson received his Purple Heart medal, presented individually by a general.

Since Iwo Jima, American concern had grown over how many Americans were dying in the war. The Joint Chiefs of Staff wondered how to tell the nation the losses were only beginning. Over half of all American battle deaths in WWII happened between June 1944 and May 1945, ending with Okinawa, which was bloodier than Iwo Jima because the rate of death per day was about the same, but the battle went on for a few more weeks.[143]

Statistics such as casualty rates were supposed to be secret, but men had seen what they had seen, and rumors of the casualty rate on Okinawa reached the Marine divisions on Hawaii as they rested after Iwo Jima and trained to attack Japan itself.

The new President Truman considered his options. There were alternatives to invasion, such as blockading Japan or bombing its transportation system. Either could cause widespread famine. Both would take time to work, during which Asian civilians would keep dying in horrendous numbers. Both might cause government overthrow, which might bring peace or might leave millions of Japanese soldiers in Asia fighting as independent units.

Japan must be convinced to surrender completely, unconditionally, and quickly. But surrendering was not something the Japanese did, and the more Japanese soldiers who died, the more the living had to keep fighting to honor them.

Could America invade Japan without Iwo Jima's and Okinawa's casualty rates? Based on the fighting so far, guesses were that for every US soldier already dead in World War II, another would be wounded or killed to take just Japan's southernmost island of Kyushu.

Based on his experiences so far, Hudson did not want to be part of that invasion. Hudson had been happy he was still alive; now he was thinking more of the men who weren't. He wrote another letter, not a happy one, about them. In the letter, he mentioned the coming operation, which he knew would be the invasion of Japan. After Iwo Jima, Hudson had no illusions about his chances of survival there. "They call Maui a rest base but we train here harder than ever waiting for the next operation." He wrote that the next operation would probably be within six months and "if you don't hear from me in a long while you know I'm aboard ship and can't write." Hudson talked about some of the men who had been killed. "I don't like to even think of some of them anymore. These fellows were all in the same platoon as I, when you live with fellows and they are gone now it seems lonely and we miss them."

To reassure his family, he wrote what were maybe not his honest thoughts at the time. "Please don't worry about me I know I can take care of myself now. God will take care of me while I'm in action." He knew now that he could handle combat, but he also knew there were times survival depended on something outside himself. After seeing who survived and who didn't survive Iwo Jima, was God, or anything outside Bill Hudson, dependable? During the battle, he kept to his Catholic faith. "I prayed every day."[144] He still has a little piece of paper with a prayer his mother sent, a prayer for help for Marines. "I prayed, and I guess maybe it worked."[145]

But later, his feelings changed. "After Iwo Jima—I lost my faith. I didn't think God should allow that to happen. That was my feeling."[146] Hudson felt sure, "No God would allow that to happen—no good God."[147]

He heard people explain the battle was not a reflection on God but a result of man's inhumanity to man. "I just said, 'I'm not going to get involved.' And I lost my faith very quickly. I didn't have to think about it. I saw things in combat that were horrible."[148] After the war, Hudson's driving force became a belief in what America stands for.

Iwo Jima was a shock to faith; not all faiths withstood the shock and the fear of death and what lay beyond. To put it in lyrics from the Civil War (which, in 1945, was in living memory), men's hearts were sifted out at Iwo Jima.

Hudson's description of the island included the statement that "If there was a hell on earth, that was it."[149] With Iwo Jima's fire of guns and flares, the cries of the dying and smells of death and sulfur, a generation raised with biblical descriptions would naturally think of Hell, and many described the island that way. In a place where a column of steam that looked like a man could form at night in cool air over a foxhole, even a calm and well-rested man might be startled. Mount Suribachi got the name "Hell's Volcano," and some said the mountain itself seemed threatening, looming over them and pressing down on them as the days went by.

The horror of the battle led another Marine in the opposite direction. Don Whipple, in the Fifth Division, became a Christian on the way to Iwo Jima. He was wounded during the invasion, but rejoined his unit. What Whipple saw on Iwo Jima drove him to prayer, and he became a pastor after the war.

Yet another Marine's faith was unmoved by the shock. William Henderson, an officer in the Fifth Division, survived thirty-six days on Iwo Jima. A Christian from the age of five, he said he found his God faithful through that time and the decades to come.

The shock was too much for faith in another god—the Japanese emperor. The Japanese worshipped their emperor, were ready to die for him, and considered their lives unworthy in comparison. The disastrous results of the war greatly disillusioned the Japanese as a people, raising the question: what god deserves such devotion?

V-E (Victory in Europe) Day finally arrived on 8 May 1945, after Hitler committed suicide in his Berlin bunker on 30 April. Army units started returning from Europe. "These men were weary in a way that no one merely reading reports could readily understand,"[150] Secretary of War Stimson later wrote, as quoted in *Downfall: The End of the Imperial Japanese Empire* by Richard B. Frank. But the men weren't going home. They would be trained to fight on the other side of the world. The reward for soldiers who survived Iwo Jima, Okinawa, and Europe was to prepare for attacking Japan in November, 1945.

Nobody had invaded Japan since Kublai Khan had failed spectacularly against the storm the Japanese called a divine wind, or *kamikaze*. After spending most of a month in combat against the Japanese, Hudson doubted his luck would hold on Japan itself. Then he heard about a program to send enlisted Marines to college to become officers. "Boy, the old light went on in my brain . . ."[151] Hudson decided he should try for the program. Dressed up in his nice khaki uniform, he interviewed before some officers. "They talked to me, and I talked to them. They evidently said, 'This guy's a candidate.'"[152]

They asked him where he would want to be assigned after getting a commission. "I said, 'The infantry, sir, because I know what the infantry's all about now. That's what I want to do.' I was lying through my teeth. And I said to myself, 'If I ever get out of here, I'm not going back in any infantry.'"[153]

Although if he had actually been assigned as an infantry platoon officer, Hudson admitted, "I'm sure I would have done it,"[154] but that at that moment, "I wanted to be far from both oceans. I wanted to be assigned to Kansas City, Missouri."[155]

The officers must have liked what they heard. Hudson qualified for the program, and in a letter on 7 May, he told his parents. "Yes this is it—I was notified a few days ago and I am leaving in a few days (very few days) and by the time you receive this letter I should be well on my way. As far as any details go I don't know much about them." After first surviving Iwo Jima, and now getting away from the Pacific, he felt, "I am the luckiest guy in the world and I can still hardly believe it yet. I am so happy about the whole thing I don't know what to do."

Hudson returned to Camp Lejeune an overseas combat veteran, older in many ways. But in his new clothes, he looked like a recruit. Some new Marines yelled at him, "You'll be sorrrry."[156] He yelled back, "I've already been sorrrry. You'll be sorrrry."[157] He arrived at Cornell University to start his degree program on the first of July, ten days before classes started: time to get familiar with the campus, have a restaurant meal, drink real milk, and eat real steak and eggs. "It was the best duty in the world."[158]

Cornell, in the middle of New York State, was close to home for Hudson and a big change from Iwo Jima. "It was summer, it was green, it was beautiful, it was peaceful, it was quiet."[159] The quiet was an important point. As Bob Greene noted in his book *Duty: A Father, His Son, and The Man Who Won the War*, quoting *Enola Gay* pilot Paul Tibbets, to that generation, silence "meant that we weren't going to get killed the next minute."[160]

For the Fourth of July, Hudson went to a big fireworks display. "The first time a firecracker went off, I dived under the picnic table. I just almost cracked. I didn't think that would happen to me, but that noise brought back so many memories so fast."[161] The transition from invading Iwo Jima in February, being wounded in March, returning to the United States in April, and coming to Cornell in July, was too much too fast. Hudson didn't stay for the fireworks. Although he had once written enthusiastically about demolitions training, "To this day I don't like noise and fireworks and guns, and I avoid it as much as possible."[162]

Overall, Hudson had a wonderful time at Cornell. He enjoyed the campus, the educational opportunity, and the break from combat. He met two other Marines who also liked gymnastics and acrobatics. Hudson's embedded shrapnel didn't stop the three of them from forming an acrobatic, tumbling, and hand-balancing team. When they had free time, they trained hard, and the acrobatic act they put together was good enough to perform in public.

There was schoolwork too, of course. Hudson didn't feel he had much aptitude for engineering, and he didn't enjoy those courses. But he knew of worse things than tests. He was supposed to pass every subject with at least a 75%. When he failed a physics class, he started taking his studies very seriously, knowing if he didn't pass he would be dropped from the program and sent back overseas.

Every Marine in the Marine Corps at that time was going to go to Japan. I mean, if you were a cook or a baker or whatever you were, that invasion was going to involve a million men. It was going to be one horrible thing.[163]

On 26 July, the Potsdam Declaration, released by the United States, the United Kingdom, and China, warned that Japan must surrender or face prompt destruction. World War I's lesson was that conditional surrenders cause follow-up wars. This time, Germany had unconditionally surrendered; so must Japan.

Radio and leaflets warned the Japanese people, in case their government didn't.

Japan did not surrender.

8

A Greater Shock than the Bombing

The only people who knew what Colonel Paul Tibbets knew were in Washington, DC or a secret town in New Mexico—or here at the bomb-loading pit on Tinian on Sunday, 5 August, writing messages on the 9,700-pound bomb, messages such as "To the people of Japan, from my friends in China."[164] (As reported by Robert and Amelia Krauss in *The 509th Remembered: A History of the 509th Composite Group as Told by the Veterans That Dropped the Atomic Bombs on Japan*.)

Tibbets, a B-29 pilot, commanded the 509th Composite Wing, the men who flew specially modified B-29s and knew that questions would get them transferred to Alaska.

Tibbets had told them, according to Krauss in *The 509th Remembered*,

You are here to take part in an effort which could end the war. Don't ask what the job is. That's a sure fire way to be transferred out. Do exactly what you are told, when you are told, and you will get along fine. Never mention this base to anybody. This means your wives, girls, sisters, family.[165]

Tibbets himself knew that what lay in the bomb pit was a super bomb to drop on Japan. He had talked to the scientists who had built the bomb with their own hands, and he'd believed them when they'd told him that the bomb now being loaded could be the knock-out punch that stopped the killing. Determined to do the job right, he prepared to fly this first mission himself. He named the aircraft that would carry the war-ending bomb the *Enola Gay* in honor of his mother. The quiet confidence she had always had in him, even when he had chosen flying over his father's hopes for his medical career, inspired Tibbets in the lonely mission entrusted to him.

With all the weight in the B-29, Tinian's runway was not really long enough. Adding to the suspense, recently wrecked B-29s lay beyond the end of the runway. Tibbets used the whole runway to build up power before climbing into the air early in the morning of 6 August. The rest of the crew would have liked to be securely in the air long before reaching the drop-off at the end.

Once in the air, Tibbets told his crew they were carrying an atomic bomb. The crewmen were interested but not shocked. They had guessed their mission had something to do with splitting atoms (it was no big secret that atoms contained tremendous energy; H. G. Wells had written about "atomic bombs" back in 1914), but they hadn't talked. The B-29 continued toward Japan.

Other B-29s accompanied the *Enola Gay* to take measurements and pictures when the bomb dropped. One B-29 went with them to Iwo Jima, then stayed there on standby. If the *Enola Gay* had trouble, Tibbets could land on Iwo Jima and move the bomb to the other B-29, using the bomb-transfer pit dug near Mount Suribachi. The island Hudson had invaded exactly twenty-four weeks before was the backup launching point for the first atomic bomb mission.

President Truman, watching the rising number of casualties in the Pacific and guessing the human cost of invading Japan itself, had been briefed only a few weeks ago that there was such a thing as an atomic bomb, and that the bomb was almost ready.

Sun Tzu said the best way to conduct war is to break the enemy's resistance without fighting.[166] Whatever the bomb was dropped on, the effect had to shatter Japanese resistance. On the advice of a committee of his strategists, Truman decided the best use of the bomb was to drop it without warning, target something not mainly civilian (such as a military town), and aim for the greatest psychological impression on the maximum number of Japanese. The B-29s were told to drop the first atomic bomb after 3 August on one of four cities: Hiroshima, Kokura, Niigata, or Nagasaki. The specific target and date would be determined by weather.

Conditions pointed to Hiroshima. As he flew over the city on 6 August, Tibbets asked his crew if they agreed the city below them was Hiroshima, their target. They agreed. Tibbets was not being rhetorical; he was thinking of a pharmacist who recognized his work could kill and therefore always had an assistant check what he was doing before mixing a prescription.

Hiroshima paid little attention to the plane. The people were used to American planes flying over at high altitude without dropping anything, such as the plane checking weather ahead of the *Enola Gay*.

At 0815 on 6 August 1945, the Little Boy atomic bomb dropped towards Hiroshima, a city containing Imperial Army training, storage, and transportation centers. The target was a T-shaped bridge. The *Enola Gay* immediately went into a steep diving turn away, adding gravitational acceleration to airspeed, making the tail-gunner feel like the last man in crack-the-whip.

Forty-three seconds after being dropped, the bomb detonated about nineteen hundred feet over Hiroshima. Little Boy was a very inefficient weapon; about ninety-eight percent of the uranium did nothing. The rest caused an explosion equivalent to fifteen thousand tons of TNT.

The scientists had told Tibbets the B-29 should survive the shock wave, but Tibbets wasn't sure. As it turned out, the shock wave felt much like the flak he had flown through over Europe. Though Tibbets had expected the bomb's power, as he flew back over the city he had just seen on approach, the sight of the scorched remains awed him.

Captain Theodore "Dutch" Van Kirk saw a flash in the airplane like a photographer's flash, and a snapping sound like a piece of sheet metal rolling. Bombardier Tom Ferebee saw pieces of buildings pulled up in the air by the wind going up the stem of the bomb. There was a feel in the mouth as when something cold touches a tooth filling, and a taste of lead. Shock waves rocking the plane felt and sounded much like being shot at from the ground.

Colonel Tibbets headed back to the base, tired but convinced that after this mission the war was finally over.

Japan did not surrender.

Estimates suggest that in Hiroshima seventy thousand to one hundred twenty thousand people were killed and more were injured.[*] The scientist in charge of the atomic bomb project, J. Robert Oppenheimer, had predicted the bomb would kill twenty thousand, assuming people would head for bomb shelters when they heard the plane approach. But it was the second air-raid alert of the day. The first had been for the plane checking Hiroshima's weather. After that plane passed and nothing happened, many people ignored the second one approaching and did not seek shelter. Similar numbers, even of civilians, had died in other battles[167]—but not from a single bomb.

Japanese leaders doubted President Truman's announcement that an atomic bomb had destroyed Hiroshima, wondering if the explosion were some trick using magnesium or liquid oxygen. They sent Japan's best atomic scientist, Yoshio Nishina, to Hiroshima to investigate what the Americans were up to.

Nishina had also been trying to build an atomic bomb. Prime Minister Tojo had given him unlimited budgets and resources, but the uranium he needed from Czechoslovakia

---

[*] See for instance "Using the Atomic Bomb - 1945," Atomic Heritage Foundation, http://www.atomicheritage.org/history/using-atomic-bomb-1945. Estimates vary widely because wartime and the sudden destruction of a city make it hard to keep good records. A figure of 80,000 dead is based on a November 1945 report (Frank, *Downfall*, 285). However, workers coming into the city for the day may mean more people were in the city when the bomb detonated, and others died less directly from burns, radiation sickness, and cancer in the following months and years. *Downfall* concludes an accurate number will never be known, but that Nagasaki's deaths were probably about half that for Hiroshima and the total number for both atomic bombs probably falls between 100,000 and 200,000. (Frank, *Downfall*, 287.)

never reached Japan, and in 1945, the B-29 raids had destroyed his research facility.

Nishina wasn't very worried. He doubted anyone, including the United States, could produce a working bomb in just a few years. Then, in Hiroshima, he recognized the results of an atomic blast. It had to have been an atomic bomb, Nishina reported, and it had destroyed the city.

Maybe the Americans did have an atomic bomb. But probably just one, or just a few, Japanese leaders decided. All Japan had to do was endure.

Emperor Hirohito was unsettled, and started to talk about an end to the war—but indecisively, when a firm statement was essential.[*] When men have been convinced to die and seen their heroes sacrifice themselves, "maybe we should quit" doesn't work. Even the emperor's word might not be enough, if the emperor were perceived as betraying his ancestors. In fact, over the next few days, some Japanese officers plotted to overthrow the government for betraying the emperor by thinking of surrender, even though one of the plotters, Pearl Harbor lead pilot Mitsuo Fuchida, had narrowly escaped being in Hiroshima the day of the bomb and had walked through the remains of the city the day after.

Americans might have been impressed by a mere demonstration of the bomb's power. But to the Japanese,

---

[*] Was Hirohito a war criminal or a figurehead? If he could make peace after the atomic bombs, why didn't he make peace before? The complexities of the Japanese government and who really ordered what to happen when, are explored in Frank, *Downfall*. The short answer seems to be, the emperor did want to fight, and even if surrendering wanted it on his own terms, but he didn't always have all the facts since his officials reported things to their own advantage.

the instant scorching of a city was just another horror of war to endure.

Radio Saipan warned the Japanese to surrender. Leaflets with pictures of the atomic cloud over Hiroshima were dropped on Japanese cities, warning them to evacuate.

Tibbets's men prepared a second bomb, Fat Man,[*] hurrying to beat several days of bad weather and to convince Japan by another bomb right after the first that the US had plenty of atomic bombs.

Some wanted to drop Fat Man on the emperor for whom the Japanese were fighting. But if their emperor died fighting, the Japanese would fight harder. Destroying Japanese headquarters would mean the war lasting until every Japanese military unit surrendered individually.

The emperor himself must surrender.

President Truman and Secretary Stimson, in their public statements, were optimistic that the bomb would bring peace quickly, if not immediately. Newspapers were already discussing peaceful uses for atomic power and reporting on how the bomb had come to be. The town of Los Alamos, New Mexico, built in the deepest possible secrecy, was suddenly world famous. In a world before internet maps and instant news reports Los Alamos had been a good hiding place; New Mexico itself was such a new state that anyone over forty or so had learned it as a territory.

The Under Secretary of War sent a congratulatory message thanking the builders of the bomb, mostly

---

[*] The two bomb names were originally Thin Man and Fat Man for Roosevelt and Churchill. Little Boy was the "little brother" of the abandoned Thin Man plutonium gunbarrel design. "Implosion Becomes a Necessity," The Manhattan Project: an interactive history, https://www.osti.gov/manhattan-project-history/Events/1942-1945/implosion_necessity.htm.

civilians, many of whom had voluntarily moved their families to a part of the country they knew nothing about, to do something they couldn't explain. They had lived with high altitude and low humidity on an unfinished Army installation, giving up a couple of years of normal life for their country. The message pointed out that none of the builders had had the complete story, but each had done his assigned job, keeping his own secrets. Now the whole world, especially the warlords of Japan, knew in full what they had only partly known.

On 8 August, Japanese warlords received another shock as the Soviet Union officially declared war on Japan. Japan had expected the Soviets to wait until America's invasion, but, breaking through Japanese lines in Manchuria, three Soviet army groups penetrated deep into Japanese-held territory.

The following day, the second atomic bomb detonated over Nagasaki. Heavier than Little Boy at 10,800 pounds, Fat Man had a core of about fourteen pounds of highly enriched plutonium 239. Ten times more efficient than the uranium bomb, Fat Man exploded like twenty-one thousand tons of TNT, killing 35,000 to 60,000 people.[168] Terrain protected some of Nagasaki, so fewer people were killed by this deadlier bomb.

If one atomic bomb hadn't stopped the Japanese, why would two? The Japanese had endured greater destruction before. The atomic bomb, however, carrying so much destruction in a single aircraft, had shock value even for a people hardened to conventional bombs and firebombs. But in case the point wasn't clear to Japan, B-29s continued firebombing. Secretary of War Stimson, not holding his breath waiting for a Japanese surrender, was actually leaving on vacation when Japan's response arrived.

Japan asked for peace on Friday, 10 August 1945 under the terms of the Potsdam Declaration, but only if Hirohito could remain as emperor. This request put a major condition on the terms, since Japan's fighting had been done in Hirohito's name. Some Japanese leaders tried to add still more conditions, saying unconditional surrender was unthinkable after so many had died for the emperor.

The United States responded, since even a willingness to consider the Potsdam terms was progress. The plutonium core of the third bomb, scheduled to be dropped 17 or 18 August near Tokyo for maximum psychological effect, was just leaving Los Alamos, but the car with the core was called back. President Truman ordered use of atomic bombs stopped until further notice, and the firebombing stopped for two days to avoid sending the wrong message during diplomatic talks.

Recognizing how many Japanese were prepared to go on fighting if the emperor were treated as a war criminal, Truman compromised, agreeing Hirohito could stay emperor if stripped of power. On 11 August, Truman answered with a change to the terms acknowledging the emperor without guaranteeing his position.

When Japan still hadn't agreed to surrender terms by 13 August, the United States, wondering what the nation that less than four years before had bombed Pearl Harbor during peace talks was planning, launched one thousand more aircraft with six thousand tons of bombs against Japan. Stimson recommended going ahead with sending the next plutonium core to Tinian.

But on Tuesday, 14 August 1945, Emperor Hirohito surrendered, announcing his decision the next day by radio to Japan. His subjects had never before heard the voice of their emperor god. This was the decisive "Stop!" and it was necessary, since even in Hiroshima's hospital, filled with the dying, anger broke out at the thought that the war had been in vain. A Hiroshima doctor reported that the word "surrender" was a greater shock to the city than the atomic bomb.[169]

Reaction to both the bomb and the surrender spread around the world.

Captured German scientists in England heard about the bomb. At first, they didn't believe it. German science, far superior to the rest of the world, hadn't been able to make a bomb; of course their enemies couldn't. Besides, from what they had learned of atomic energy, an atomic bomb wouldn't fit on a plane. This must be something else. But they found they were wrong. For German scientists, the shock was not that a city had been destroyed; it was that their confidence in superior German science lay shattered.

In Nanking, citizens feared Japan's surrender was a false rumor. Many stayed in hiding while Japanese soldiers evacuated.

In Santa Fe, New Mexico's capital, the mood was excitement. *Now we can tell all our stories!*

Los Alamos scientists' wives and families were proud of what their men had accomplished, but annoyed with themselves that they hadn't guessed.

In one Girl Scout camp, campers gathered around to pray for those people guilty of having built such a bomb, unaware that one woman there was from Los Alamos.

Project leader Oppenheimer had no apologies, considering it both necessary and right to build a bomb that had won the war. But he hoped that even a fraction of the money spent would now be used in peacetime for science benefiting human life.

Members of the military celebrated being allowed to go on living. One Marine corporal quoted in Smith's book

Iwo Jima said, "The A-bomb was quite a thrill for us. . . . We were told we were going to hit the southern island of Kyushu and to be prepared to lose ninety-eight percent on the initial landing."[170]

Another Marine corporal (and Medal of Honor recipient) quoted in Smith's *Iwo Jima* observed,

> You know, your averages do run out and with two hundred fifty thousand civilians the Japanese had trained, women, children twelve and up, with every kind of weapon you could think of, an ax or sharpened bamboo or whatever; they were going to fight us to the last person, so I'm not sure my number wouldn't have come up.[171]

An Army B-29 bombardier Smith quoted was glad "we saved all those lives that would have been lost invading Japan by dropping the atomic bomb."[172]

A B-29 navigator Smith quoted said, "I think in the long run it saved more lives than were lost. . . . T]he Japanese were not in the mood to surrender."[173]

A paratrooper in Europe was grateful. "We knew we were on our way to Japan. I had a friend in high school who went to the South Pacific. He died within six weeks. . . . I got to come home because of [the *Enola Gay* crew] . . ."[174]

Fred Haynes, a captain at Iwo Jima, and later a major general, spoke for the men of Iwo Jima:

> It was only the threat of the destruction of their civilization in the form of the atom bomb that finally broke Japan's commitment to fighting the Americans to the last man. . . .The invasion of Japan proper, if it had actually happened, would have been a bloodbath for Americans and Japanese alike

too hideous to contemplate. When the Japanese finally surrendered in August, I think I can speak for every man in the regiment when I say that we were euphoric, as if a death sentence had been lifted.[175]

A Japanese boy living near Hiroshima later moved to America and opened a business, where he one day hosted Paul Tibbets and told him that his father had said "the end of the war spared the lives of 'men, women, children' all over Japan."[176]

Fred Bock, the usual pilot of the plane flown by Charles Sweeney to drop Fat Man, heard later from the president of Toyota that he owed his life to the atomic bombs; as a sixteen-year-old Japanese boy in 1945, his job would have been to wrap himself in high explosives and take as many Americans with him as he could.[177]

Pearl Harbor lead pilot Mitsuo Fuchida, once convinced the emperor genuinely wished to surrender, was glad to obey. Fuchida later became a Christian, and his children became Americans. Within fifteen years, he was a guest in Paul Tibbets's house.

Bill Hudson, studying to become a Marine officer, said "it was like someone took a steel band off my head. It was over."[178]

President Truman's statement after Hiroshima explained that the force powering the sun had been released against those who brought war to the Far East. In his memoirs, he wrote that he'd never had any doubt the bomb should be used.

American troops landed in Japan and took over on 28 August. General MacArthur, in charge of occupying Japan, created a democracy with a constitution requiring political freedom and outlawing war. To American surprise and to

Japanese benefit, the former enemies cooperated with American occupying forces after the war, in much the same way Japanese prisoners had during the war.

Emperor Hirohito was stripped of power but allowed to live and keep the title of emperor, so he went back to studying marine biology. On New Year's Day of 1946, on MacArthur's request, he issued a statement denying that he was a living god.

The Japanese signed the surrender document on Sunday, 2 September 1945, on the USS Missouri in Tokyo Bay under the same flag that had flown over the US Capitol on the Sunday Pearl Harbor had been attacked. An American victory had happened without Japanese national suicide. However, Japan continued fighting the Soviet Union till 12 September, losing 80,000 Japanese to 8,000 Soviets, and seventy years later, Japan and Russia still have not signed a peace agreement.

Tsunezo Wachi, the former garrison commander of Iwo Jima, who escaped almost certain death by being ordered back to Japan, narrowly avoided death twice more in the final months of the war. He believed his life was spared for a reason and felt a debt to the five thousand subordinates and friends he'd left on Iwo Jima. After the war, Wachi presented a letter to a Marine officer, explaining his desire to become a Buddhist priest and pray and mourn for those souls. Wachi offered his former enemies "any information I possess regarding the defence of Iwo Jima against air attack, if the American authorities so desire it."[179] The positive response Wachi received surprised him.

I was deeply impressed. It actually marked the very first step of my devotion to the problems of Iwo Jima and to this day I appreciate the thoughtfulness and friendship rendered me by them right after the dreadful war.[180]

Wachi returned to his family that autumn wearing a Buddhist habit instead of the Imperial Japanese Navy uniform.

Now that the dreadful war was over, Marines who had volunteered or were drafted for the "duration of national emergency" found they were done. They had survived. They could go home to their families. They could start their own families. They could see their children and grandchildren. But not the next day; America had taken a while to get ready to fight, and demobilization when the fighting was over also took time. Hudson's division, the Fourth, was the first Marine division after the war to return to the United States and be deactivated—in November, the month it had been scheduled to invade Japan.

In some ways, the division had it easy. The Fourth spent only twenty-one months overseas (other divisions spent twenty-six to thirty) and saw only sixty-three days of combat. The Fourth's training happened in Maui, Hawaii, and the division never had jungle fighting, malaria, jungle rot, or excessive heat. But the Fourth was part of more violent combat than any other Marine division. Its sixty-three days of combat on Roi-Namur, Saipan, Tinian, and Iwo Jima contained more action than months of jungle fighting, and in just over a year, the Fourth made four bitterly opposed beachheads. Six Marines of the Fourth Division received the Medal of Honor for Iwo Jima.

In November, Hudson was still in the officer program at Cornell, but now he knew he would not have to go back overseas as a Marine officer. "Fortunately, the atomic bomb went off, the war ended, and I got discharged."[181] November was the month he received the Bronze Star award, as recognition for what he had been doing when he had been wounded. "It was a proud moment for me that I will always remember." The officer cadets assembled to see a Navy captain in charge of the officer program present him with the award. The cadets were informed that when an enemy bunker had been causing heavy casualties, Hudson had gone up and "engaged the enemy with hand grenades and, despite a painful wound suffered earlier in the attack, relentlessly continued until he had destroyed the bunker."

Hudson receives the Bronze Star award

Wounds attract attention. When a soldier is wounded, for him the action stops. Others want to hear his story, and may have time to find out what happened. A wounded soldier might get an award for something he did better many other times unnoticed.

Hudson downplayed the grenade duel: "He didn't have a weapon. He didn't have a pistol or a rifle, but he had a grenade. And for that little operation, somebody wrote it up, and I got the Bronze Star." The award meant a lot to Hudson, but perhaps felt misplaced compared with all he had seen. Where uncommon valor is common, recognizing one deed among many seems wrong. Many heroic events happened when nobody had time to notice, or nobody lived to remember them. Yet recognizing one deed is better than recognizing none.

9

A Marine Defends Los Alamos

Hudson stayed at Cornell for about a year. With the pressure of being sent overseas off, Hudson enjoyed going to class, and his grades got better. Hudson could have returned to Cornell as a civilian, but wanted to stay closer to home, so he used the GI Bill to enroll at New York University.

In the summer of 1946, while waiting for his discharge papers from the Marine Corps after Cornell, Hudson spent a day in Brooklyn guarding prisoners who were cleaning up garbage. With his Thompson submachine gun, he announced to them, "I'm a combat veteran. I just got off Iwo Jima, and I know how to use this thing."[182] If they tried to escape, "I'm going to shoot you. Because if you get away, they'll delay my discharge, and I want to get out of the Marine Corps now."[183] The prisoners looked at him and decided, "The crazy Marine might shoot us,"[184] and gave him no trouble.

When his discharge papers came through, he went through the processing line and finally heard the words, "You're all through, discharged."[185] The Marines paid for transportation home, which in Hudson's case was a nickel for the subway from Brooklyn to Manhattan. Hudson was happy to take off his uniform for the last time. "Don't get me wrong—I loved the Marine Corps, but I didn't love it enough to stay in. I did my job, and the Marine Corps used me for what they needed me for. But I wanted to be a civilian."[186]

Hudson had known for a long time that he wanted to be a physical education teacher. Being a career Marine didn't interest him; he had no desire to be an engineer or a Marine lieutenant. In later years, as Iwo Jima faded into memory, the option of staying in the Marines didn't seem so bad. "Looking back . . . maybe it would have been a good deal."[187] But he had no real regrets. "I did what I wanted to do and I was very happy about what I did. I've had a very good life."[188] Hudson has spent most of the rest of that good life far from the coast in a town built to be safe from naval attack: Los Alamos, New Mexico.

Los Alamos had been, and remained, very cosmopolitan for a Southwestern town of its size. Scientists from England, Poland, Switzerland, Canada, Germany, the United States, and Austria had worked with American soldiers, Pueblo Indians, and Hispanics. During the war scientists even had to be reminded not to speak European languages in Santa Fe.

For decades before the war, physicists from many countries had worked together trying to understand the atom. By the time war broke out, scientists on both sides knew an atomic bomb was a possibility. The former colleagues became competing teams racing to build a bomb.

Top names in physics were on both sides. Nobel Prize winner Werner Heisenberg, known for the Heisenberg Uncertainty Principle, led the German effort. Yoshio Nishina, in charge of the Japanese effort, for years had worked with Niels Bohr in Denmark, and coauthored the Klein-Nishina formula. Los Alamos had its British and American scientists, but many of its leaders came from Europe. European refugees got Los Alamos started because American scientists had been too busy working on the new technology of radar, a high priority for the war and too sensitive to trust to foreign scientists.

Though European scientists warned in 1939 that German research already led Allied research by two years, it was hard for non-scientists to take them seriously. After all, these were foreigners talking about an atom bomb, which was science fiction—like space travel. And they came from Europe. Could they really want to build a bomb to use on their own countries?

The answer was yes: a bomb would destroy less of Europe than Hitler would, and the refugees feared what Heisenberg's team might build for Hitler. Many European refugee scientists were Jewish by birth if not religion. Some lost family members in the Holocaust. (One reason Germany's atomic bomb program failed was that so many nuclear physicists were Jewish that the whole field was frowned on as "Jewish physics.")

When restrictions on Italian Jews grew under Mussolini, Italian physicist Enrico Fermi escaped with his Jewish wife and family through Sweden, where he had been invited to receive the Nobel Prize, and came to America. The American consulate was careful to make sure Italian immigrants were of sound mind; to get his visa, the Nobel Prize winner had to add 15 and 27, and divide 29 by 2.

It was Fermi and his friends who wrote the letter warning the President of the United States what European science had learned. They got the letter signed by another European refugee, Albert Einstein. The letter explained that recent work on uranium showed that a single bomb of an extremely powerful new type could be carried into a port by a boat and destroy the whole port. (They didn't know yet the bomb could be made light enough to be delivered by air.)

Roosevelt read the letter and agreed. "This requires action!"[189]

With a push from British scientists confirming that an atomic bomb could be built, the result was Los Alamos, an Army installation thrown together in an unpopulated area, surrounded by land the government already owned. A railroad stop was close at hand near Santa Fe, and a road wound its way up to the site, but the landscape of a mesa backed by mountains allowed tight access control. As the project took over an existing ranch school, some power, water, fuel, and housing for scientists was available.

Arriving scientists were sent to a small office in Santa Fe, which arranged for famous physicists to get to Los Alamos under assumed names. "Nicholas Baker" was the Nobel Prize-winning Danish scientist Niels Bohr who developed the Bohr model of the atom. Enrico Fermi, as in the element fermium, was Eugene Farmer. The name for Arthur Compton (yet another Nobel Prize winner) for whom the Compton effect is named, was Mr. Comas on one coast and Mr. Comstock on the other; he'd had to decide quickly what to answer when someone asked his name on a flight from California to New York. Titles and fields of expertise also had to be disguised. Renowned scientists couldn't call themselves "Doctor" or "physicist."

Within Los Alamos, however, physicists and chemists were unofficially called "fizzlers and stinkers."[190]

The scientists found the restrictions irritating and inconvenient, even though they themselves had decided the project needed strict secrecy. Sometimes they were a bit casual in their compliance. In 1944, the post bulletin had to remind Los Alamos residents to stop when ordered by military police, if they didn't want .45 caliber bullet holes in their vehicles. Scientists whose daily job was questioning the laws of physics would loudly argue about rules they didn't see the sense of. One scientist insisted the secret document he forgot to lock up actually helped national security; it was so full of mistakes an enemy would only get disinformation from it.

Even the name "Los Alamos" was classified information, so the place was called Site Y, Project Y, or, by those living at the 7,200-foot altitude, "The Hill." The town was not shown on maps, and those who lived there couldn't vote. Since babies couldn't officially be born in Los Alamos, they were recorded as born in the Santa Fe post office box where regular mail from Los Alamos went.

The original plan was for thirty scientists to move in. Plans changed, and during the war about six thousand people called Los Alamos home, and that number doubled over the next fifteen years. Over the years the median age rose, along with the percentage of Los Alamos residents who had lived there at least five years, but the town remained unusual. Statistics such as half the male population having an advanced degree, high school graduation percentages in the high 90s, and half the unemployment rate and twice the household income as the rest of the state made Los Alamos a great place to live. Of course, with twice as many employed in science, engineering, and computers as sales jobs,

Los Alamos career options were somewhat limited—but far from nonexistent, as Hudson proved.

Hudson had received the bachelor's and master's degrees he needed for teaching when he heard Los Alamos needed teachers. Hudson didn't know much about Los Alamos, but he knew the bomb the scientists had built there had ended the war. Many scientists had stayed on in Los Alamos, researching further questions about atoms and national security, and these scientists wanted their children well educated.

Right after the war was a great time to be a scientist, especially a physicist. Scientists are rarely popular in school and distantly respected after that. But after the war, physicists were suddenly superstars, credited with winning the war through their brilliance. Suddenly, everyone wanted wisdom from those amazing physicists; they became very popular as dinner guests. Of course, these scientists could be rather odd, and their international backgrounds certainly stood out in New Mexico. They had unique and varied interests not limited to science. Wartime scientists' hobbies included playing drums or piano, riding horses, and studying philosophy. They lifted weights and ate health foods (before health food stores were common) or hunted bears to bring a bearskin back to Oxford. They searched for ancient relics, climbed mountains, dug mines, square danced, sang, and played in an orchestra. If they hadn't been a little peculiar, said one wartime scientist's wife, life in Los Alamos would have been less fun.

General Groves, the Army officer in charge of Los Alamos, once called the scientists "expensive crackpots."

"But I am an exception," said Enrico Fermi. "I am perfectly normal."[191]

"We were all crackpots,"[192] said his wife Laura.

Many of the big names in physics who built the bomb with their own hands, not knowing whether Los Alamos had a future, had returned to their pre-war jobs at universities by the time Hudson arrived. But many others had stayed and management had passed from the Army to the new Atomic Energy Commission. New scientists were coming to Los Alamos to investigate what else atomic energy could do, drawn by the place's reputation and opportunities. The original Los Alamos was the physics version of creating a football team from everyone in the Pro Football Hall of Fame; thirteen Los Alamos scientists had already been or later would be awarded the Nobel Prize for physics. Being part of Los Alamos even after the war was exciting for a young physicist.

Hudson, on the other hand, was impressed by the Los Alamos dress code. By 1940s' standards, the Los Alamos dress was very casual. Enough lumberjack shirts and blue jeans were ordered by mail that any spies would be convinced the town was full of cowboys, said one Los Alamos wife. Seeing a picture of faculty without neckties, Hudson thought if Los Alamos was that informal, "Sign me up!"

Hudson set out for Los Alamos in 1949 to teach physical education. He had a special pass to get through the town's gate. Four years after the war, the town was still secured, but at least its existence was no longer a secret. Besides, unlike scientists, Hudson was used to gates, passes, code names, and being told he couldn't say certain things in his letters.

Hudson found Los Alamos was not the desert many expect of a New Mexico town. At seven thousand feet above sea level, stars shone bright and close. Los Alamos is surrounded by mountains and can get snowfalls of several feet; the wartime scientists had dammed up a stream in one canyon to make a skating rink. Los Alamos was a wonderful place for a fitness enthusiast like Hudson.

Physical fitness was easy to encourage when there were so many possibilities and the population was young and active. During the war, most of the scientists were only a few years older than Hudson (somebody was always having to explain why they shouldn't be drafted) and the average age hadn't risen much yet. Local fishing, skiing, hiking, hunting, horse-riding, ice-skating, and other attractions had been and still were popular with scientists mentally exhausted from laboratory work. Over the years, many scientists joined Hudson in organizing and promoting athletic events.

Hudson enjoyed hiking the mountains where Enrico Fermi had hiked and fished (not very successfully, according to fellow physicist Emilio Segre, as Fermi unscientifically refused to let experience change his theories of how fish ought to behave). Nearby were the ancient trails and ruins of Bandelier National Monument, where scientists hiking with Niels Bohr had to warn him that skunks—unknown in Europe—should be left alone.

Hudson made his home where men world famous for their intelligence had worked and played, and his job was educating their next generation. Teaching high schoolers in a town with so much education per capita might have been intimidating if he hadn't been a Marine, but a combat veteran could keep order in a classroom.

Los Alamos had plenty of work remaining, since physics had shown that more powerful weapons were possible. Many people had hoped the atomic bomb would bring lasting peace because everyone would be too afraid to start a war. Yet Los Alamos had been only one, and not the first one, of the efforts to build an atomic bomb. World

War II had shown that if a weapon were possible to build, somebody would try it, and everyone else would have to join in so as not to be at the builder's mercy.

The question was not whether bigger and better weapons would be built, but rather who would have them first. Germany and Japan were defeated, but other enemies were on the horizon. In 1949, the Soviet Union used information from spy contacts in Los Alamos during the war to explode their own atomic weapon. Although the Soviet Union under Stalin officially had been an ally in World War II, in the closing days of the war, Stalin used his spies' information to guess when the United States and Japan would make peace and draw Japan's boundary lines. Before that could happen, Stalin seized land in Asia, and over two million Japanese became Soviet prisoners and forced laborers. Over three hundred thousand never returned.

The quick end to the war kept the Soviet Union out of Japan itself, so Japan avoided the fate of Germany. Germany, with its capital Berlin, was sliced into East and West between the Soviet Union and the western allies (United States, Britain, and France), with the Berlin Wall preventing East Germans from escaping. West Berlin stayed free because of the Berlin Airlift, which had ended in 1949— because the United States and Britain succeeded in flying food and supplies to their recent enemies, past the blockade of their recent ally. No direct American-Soviet war was declared, then or later, but for the next fifty years, America and the Soviet Union backed opposite sides in many conflicts, and many predicted a World War III of America against the Soviet Union. Once more, the United States saw an urgent need to have weapons better than those of its enemies, but in the hope of never actually using them.

Better weapons were known to be possible. Little Boy and Fat Man had been two versions of the fission-type atomic bomb.[*] During the war, Los Alamos had considered another type of bomb, much more powerful, a fusion bomb that used a fission bomb to set it off. Since the design was more complicated, the scientists had shelved it until after the war, when they would have more time to study the problem. After the 1949 Soviet atomic test, Los Alamos got busy researching this third type, which became the hydrogen bomb, also known as a thermonuclear device or nuclear weapon.

Some of the scientists who had worked on the atomic bomb were not happy with the effort to build nuclear weapons because the more powerful the weapon, the harder it would be to restrict the blast to military targets. The debate continued over the years, with nuclear physicists on both sides, and it eventually intertwined with the anti-war movement of the 1960s and spread backward to question whether the atomic bomb should have been built at all. But even I. I. Rabi, one of the prominent wartime scientists who by the 1980s felt that politicians had misused the discoveries, did not regret his work in the 1940s. It was a different time, he said; there was a genuine need for an atomic bomb against Nazism. Other scientists, meanwhile, remained proud of their work to end the war, though those who were

---

[*] Little Boy was two pieces of uranium shot together to make a critical mass. It was a simple design, but uranium-235 was in short supply.

Fat Man was a ball of plutonium, compressed by explosives into a smaller ball dense enough to be the critical mass needed for reaction. Plutonium, a man-made element not found in nature, in the end was cheaper to produce than uranium, and the Fat Man design was safer in case of an accident. Plutonium was first made in 1940, but just five years later, the Manhattan Project produced enough for several bombs. The main problem with plutonium was figuring out how to shape the explosives around it and set them off at the same time so the plutonium ball would compress everywhere at the same instant.

university professors during 1960s anti-war protests probably did not advertise their backgrounds.

At first, Hudson paid little attention to anti-nuclear protests in Los Alamos. He thought, given human history, war obviously was going to keep happening. He had seen war, hadn't enjoyed it, and didn't want to glorify it. He had done his part, and now he saw no reason to be around guns. When his wife wanted to buy a BB gun for their boy, he agreed the boy should learn to shoot, but told his wife she'd be doing the teaching, and he'd be somewhere else.

For thirty-three years, Hudson stored camping equipment in his Marine sea bag while he taught and coached Los Alamos elementary and high school swimming. He started the high school swimming team and the Los Alamos Aquatomics and built what was probably the best swimming program in New Mexico (both boys' and girls' swim teams won the state title six out of the ten years Hudson coached both teams). In 1974, he founded the Los Alamos Triathlon, the oldest continuing triathlon in the country. With his wife, he started a gymnastics school with over 250 children involved—a large fraction of the town's children. Hudson got to know the children of the scientists, and through them the scientists themselves, even the Lab's director.

Hudson himself raised four children, one of whom spent time in the Marines stationed in Japan. After retiring from teaching in Los Alamos, Hudson lived on an island again briefly, teaching physical education for a year in Puerto Rico.

Returning to Los Alamos, Hudson taught fitness skills to Laboratory employees. Hudson was an example of the benefits of physical fitness, and could teach out-of-shape beginners to build up slowly, warning them not to expect fitness from a single workout. Over the years, he ran five marathons, including the Marine Corps Marathon; ran up Colorado's 14,114-foot Pike's Peak three times; ran down and up the Grand Canyon; and bicycled five hundred miles across Oregon in seven days.

On his fiftieth birthday, he ran fifty miles; on his six-tieth birthday, he ran sixty miles. At sixty-five, he was part of a relay team swimming the English Channel. At seventy, he did seventy laps on the track, seventy laps in the pool, and lifted a seventy-pound dumbbell overhead with one arm. At eighty, he walked eighty minutes, swam eighty laps, and lifted an eighty-pound weight overhead with one arm. All this with shrapnel in his hand and arm.

Because of his shrapnel, Hudson qualified for a 10% disability payment of $13 per month at the time he was dis-charged from the Marines. Hudson was almost apologetic that he still got the monthly payment, that he should be considered "disabled" when he could bench-press 175 pounds, tumble, and do handstands. However, as he says, "I left a little blood, sweat, and tears over there for it."[193]

As he became a father and grandfather, Hudson saw generations, seeming younger than his generation had ever been, growing up ignorant of war and history. He saw wars fought in Korea, Vietnam, and Iraq with no decision of what victory would be and no clear understanding of what the world should look like afterward. Most of the fighting over the years was technically not war; nobody wanted to declare that war had started, and nobody was sure when to declare the fighting over. "Police actions" with no agreed-on goals were easy to start but hard to finish.

For years, Hudson remembered the Marine Corps mainly on the Marine Corps Birthday (10 November) and on the anniversaries of the 19 February invasion and his wounding on 15 March. But as time passed, he looked back over what he had experienced. He started reading books, getting reports, and talking to other Iwo Jima veterans. "When I realized how tough it was, I got scared. I thought . . . 'Did I go through this?' It was unbelievable."[194]

Hudson slowly realized there was not only a need for somebody (Marines, to start with) to know how to fight, but also for people to know why and when to fight—and when not to. Hudson began giving presentations to schools and later to other groups. In schools, he could reach the age group that finds war most exciting. He taught about war from the authority of experience, warning that war is a terrible thing. War is not Hollywood. For instance, you don't fall on a hand grenade, you throw it back. You hide from it. You tell your other buddies to hide from it. War destroys hopes, dreams, and people, especially young men. War is also part of the history of the world; all of history holds only short periods without war. War is a miserable thing, and you don't do miserable things without good reasons. But atrocities such as those the Japanese committed have to be stopped. So you fight fast and get it over with. You do the job completely so you don't have to do it over again.

To Hudson's generation, these points were obvious. But what he saw as facts, the next generation saw as arguable opinions: war isn't inevitable; we just need better communication. The children of that next generation weren't even arguing; they simply had no idea what he was talking about. Why, they wondered, would you go live on an island and shoot at people—it sounds uncomfortable and probably racist, too.

The more Hudson talked, the deeper he realized the ignorance went. American youth weren't the only ones who didn't understand; a young Japanese lady he talked to was interested that he had seen the Japanese soldier who wounded him. She was shocked to learn that Hudson had then killed the man. Somewhat shocked himself at her shock, Hudson wondered if she'd expected him to ask the man to tea.

Hudson questioned how much students were learning of the history he and his generation had made. His generation had wanted to spare themselves and their listeners the painful details of their war experience, assuming their descendants would learn all they needed to know in school. After finding the result was decades of ignorance about World War II, ignorance passed on and magnified from generation to generation, veterans started talking about their experiences, trying to correct the record while they were around to do so.

During the 1990s, veteran protests and objections resulted in the Smithsonian Institution cancelling an exhibit about the *Enola Gay*. Veterans complained the exhibit focused too much on the Japanese as hapless victims of the atomic bomb rather than as the ones who started the war. On the other hand, in 1994 the Post Office rescinded a commemorative stamp for the first time ever. The stamp showed a mushroom cloud, which Japanese officials and President Clinton found objectionable. Hudson was especially galled when the White House picked December 8th, 1994, to announce rescinding the stamp, 53 years to the day after America declared war on Japan in response to Pearl Harbor.

In 1995, for the fiftieth anniversary of Iwo Jima, Hudson had a reunion with his platoon sergeant Manuel Martinez and also invited a friend who brought along another friend interested in military history. The friend's friend turned out to be James N. Pritzker, a lieutenant colonel in the National Guard and the billionaire founder of a military history library.

Pritzker sent Hudson and his wife tickets to a 1998 Marine Corps Ball. Here the former PFC Bill Hudson got introduced to the 31st Commandant of the Marine Corps. (Hudson's division commander at Iwo Jima, Clifton Cates, had been the 19th Commandant.) To put the Commandant in perspective to one small boy, Hudson explained this privilege was "better than meeting Santa Claus." Hudson also met Joe Rosenthal, the photographer of the famous Mount Suribachi flag-raising picture. Rosenthal said he had, like Hudson, landed on Blue Beach originally, but there had been too much going on for someone armed with just a camera. Rosenthal went back to the ship and landed somewhere else and ended up on Mount Suribachi with the Fifth Division.

Hudson continued giving presentations to various groups about World War II, the war in the Pacific, and Iwo Jima. He lectured to classes of future Marines at the Marine Military Academy in Texas, where the Pritzker Foundation had him hand out their scholarship awards.

As a Los Alamos resident, he often ended up talking about the atomic bombs. He surprised any listeners who expected an apology. "I thank the scientists who made the bombs," he would say, "and I thank President Harry Truman for having the moral courage to make the decision to use them." At a presentation in 1995, Hudson even gave an introduction for the weaponeer of the B-29 that carried the Fat Man bomb.

Hudson was defending the scientists, and maybe the Los Alamos scientists were in need of a Marine to defend them. Since Einstein, physicists had been revered for understanding the secret workings of the world. They were heroes after the war for bringing Japan to the surrender that the entire US military had been fighting for. But in the decades since then, the anti-war and anti-nuclear movement, along with Hollywood, had turned the image of physicists and chemists into brilliant but cold and inhumane men often in league with insane generals who enjoyed blowing things up.

Scientists often were not a help to their own case, since they prided themselves on understanding the complexities of a situation and being unwilling to make a definitive statement without at least an estimate of the limits of error. Often they sounded more doubtful than they were. Besides, long hours in a laboratory don't contribute to interpersonal skills, and the traits that make a world-class scientist rarely include great communication abilities.

"Ending the war by dropping the atomic bombs saved my life." Hudson has a direct way of explaining things. A blunt, straight-talking Marine, a common foot soldier who happened to be in the Pacific at the time, who had little inherent reason for liking scientists other than living in Los Alamos, turned out to be a good spokesman for his neighbors.

> The facts are that Japan started the war, and the United States ended it. We used two atomic bombs against Japan, and that action brought a quick end to the war that went on for five bloody years. Over 290,000 Americans were killed and over 570,000 Americans were wounded in WWII. In my mind, these numbers alone would justify the use of the bombs.

Hudson has little patience for charges that the bombs were an act of racism against the Japanese. An invasion would have cost far more Japanese deaths, he says, and Japan would probably have been divided like Germany.

Hudson had the background the scientists lacked to cut through pet theories of history and sociology. Academic arguments didn't seem so realistic beside the personal experience of a combat-educated Marine who had faced the enemy and still carried shrapnel from the experience.

In 1999, encouraged by Pritzker and other history-minded friends, Hudson self-published his collection of Iwo Jima memories and memorabilia under the title "Once a Marine, Always a Marine." The book included many of the letters his mother had saved, which he realized were a priceless glimpse into what a 19-year-old felt at the time. Over half a century later, Hudson admits,

> The difficult part of writing a personal military history is I am writing it now, through the mind of a mature adult. I am trying to think back when I was a young Marine, realizing that a young person doesn't have the life experiences that I have now.

Those life experiences, however, are built on that time as a young Marine. Hudson saw that his experience on Iwo Jima made him who he is today; no other period in his life—including marriage, divorce, and children—has so affected him.

Another of his generation, Paul Tibbets, as quoted in Greene's book *Duty*, spoke about the men of World War II:

> A time like that comes along only once in a lifetime—if that. You are literally risking your life every day, and you're doing it with the men who are next to you. You form friendships during days and nights like those that nothing and no one in your entire life will ever match.

Please pay attention: The reason those years mean so much to so many of us is that it is the one time in your life that you are absolutely proud of what you are doing, and you are absolutely proud of your friends and what they are doing. It's a relationship of man to man.[195]

Hudson looked at books, photographs, and letters, and thought about things he hadn't thought about for 50 years. He didn't especially want to discover whether he had blocked out memories that were too traumatic, but he tried anyway, so as to search out exactly what had happened, to bring the history to his readers "as accurately and truthfully as possible." Hudson dedicated the book to all the Marines of his platoon, both those who came back and those who didn't, but most of all to Manuel Martinez, "the bravest, most courageous person I have ever known," a "true hero, and patriot."

The words were no casual compliment. Hudson considers Martinez his personal hero, ahead of General George Patton (who ought to have been a Marine, Hudson thinks.) At one reunion, a captain who had been wounded in the first six hours on Iwo Jima questioned how Martinez survived the whole battle without even being wounded. He suggested to Martinez that hiding was the only way to get through the battle unwounded. Martinez's son was at the reunion, and hearing the captain's words, "was about ready to tear him apart."[196]

Hudson, an eyewitness of Martinez's actions in battle, reacted intensely when he heard what was said. "I wish his son would have torn him apart. The captain implied that Martinez was hiding because he wasn't wounded. Nothing could be further from the truth."[197]

Hudson's return to Iwo Jima in memory eventually led him to return in person. The island the Marines took has not been a US possession since 1968, when the United States gave Iwo Jima back to Japan. Neither is it an ordinary piece of Japanese land. No flags fly on Iwo Jima except for the American flag, one day a year. When the island was returned, the condition was that the Marines have access to Iwo Jima forever. The Marines use that privilege to conduct memorial tours coordinated between Japan and America. On the day of the annual memorial tour, they fly the American flag.

Hudson saw an ad for the one-day tour in a Marine magazine. His first reaction was "Maybe I don't want to go back there."[198] But then he thought he might not have another opportunity. In 2001, he stood again on Iwo Jima.

> What was really fascinating was when we landed on Iwo Jima it was a black rock. When I went back to Iwo Jima in 2001, it was green. We were flying in, and I saw that green island, and I said, 'That's not the same island I was on.' It was *green*. Even Suribachi was *green*.[199]

Hudson had hoped to walk through the area where he had fought, but he couldn't. The overgrowth was too dense.

The Marine veterans had a brief period that day to meet Japanese veterans. The veterans had no common language except a momentary handshake and respect for a fellow man who had experienced the same event. Hudson traded his Fourth Marine Division cap for one of theirs that said "Iwo Jima" in Japanese. The veteran he traded with wrote Hudson a letter in Japanese, which Hudson had translated. Hudson found this man had held out on the island and stayed in his cave for two weeks after the battle, going out at night and stealing food from the Army Air Force. Another Japanese veteran Hudson met had directed mortar fire on Hudson's outfit. This time, Hudson shot back with a camera.

Hudson also made one of the closest friends he has today, Rosa Ogawa, the daughter of Japanese Navy captain Tsunezo Wachi, who designed Japanese defenses on Iwo Jima and who spent the rest of his life working to heal the wounds of Iwo Jima. In contrast to Hudson's loss of his Catholic faith after Iwo Jima, Wachi, though a Buddhist priest, recommended to his wife that she and the children should learn Christianity. Wachi himself was baptized by a Jesuit friend shortly before his death in 1990.

Hudson learned that even after half a century, the Japanese wished for Americans to return battle souvenirs. As president of Japan's Iwo Jima association, Wachi explained to many Marines how much the families of Japanese soldiers would appreciate having the souvenirs returned. His courteous pleas moved many Marines, despite their memories of what they had gone through to get the souvenirs, and they returned items they had kept for decades. Some received deeply appreciative responses from the families who received the items.

Hudson returned some pictures and the flag he took from a helmet, sending them in care of Ogawa. He became good friends with Ogawa in spite of her father's wartime position, because of her father's post-war work. When Hudson's wife Maureen, a former professional ice skater, died, Ogawa honored her by sending from Japan a memorial donation for ice skaters.

During the tour, the Canadian History Channel interviewed Hudson and other veterans for a video about Iwo Jima, and later sent him a copy of the video. Since the video was not aired publicly on US television, Hudson added it to his personal efforts to educate American audiences, showing the video in yearly talks commemorating the invasion of Iwo Jima.

Revisiting Iwo Jima gave Hudson the idea for a memorial run up the five-hundred-foot volcano that had taken Marines five days to ascend in 1945. Hudson was seventy-six the next year when he raised ten thousand dollars for

Hudson on Mount Suribachi, 2002

the Iwo Jima Museum by running up Mount Suribachi in seventeen minutes. He planted a small flag at the top.

Mount Suribachi looks different now. So do Hiroshima and Nagasaki, which, far from being wastelands, are today thriving cities with multiple times their 1945 populations. So is Los Alamos, now with Los Alamos National Laboratory—which, along with weapons research, conducts other basic research, from studies of outer space to fingerprinting technology to human genome mapping. Even the weapons research spins off whole fields of study such as computer modeling. There is great respect in Los Alamos for those first scientists who built the atomic bombs with their own hands. The laboratory draws scientists from around the world, and Los Alamos children grow up knowing that finding a job in their home town means competing in the hard sciences against world-class PhDs.

In recent years, Hudson invited to his home a Japanese swim team visiting Los Alamos. He was happy to host them, to have lived through the war with their grandfathers, to be alive and sharing with them a common interest in physical fitness. In 2005, Los Alamos honored its Marine by adding Hudson and his wife to the list of Living Treasures of Los Alamos, in appreciation of Hudson's years of dedication to the community's fitness and his talks on World War II.

Hudson wears his Fourth Division cap with great pride. Of the twenty-five thousand men in his division at Iwo Jima, Hudson is one of maybe a thousand still alive.[200] As a survivor of the decades as well as of Iwo Jima, he is a celebrity among today's Marines, who are flattered to meet an actual living Iwo Jima Marine and hear his story. Approaching ninety years of age, Hudson is grateful that he is still living. He feels the limits of the human body and says that if he reaches ninety, his athletic celebration will be to lift a beer and laugh.

Having seen the worst of war, Hudson refuses to glorify it, but sees honor in taking up the responsibility to fight when necessary.

> I still think about my time in the Marines, and how that experience influenced my life today. It was an honorable time for me to be a Marine, and I am proud that I will be a Marine as long as I live.
>
> If there was any such thing as a good war, no matter how many millions of people were killed, World War II was a good war. We liberated millions of people to freedom. We freed people from tyranny, and we wiped out the dictatorship of Adolf Hitler and Hirohito, the Japanese emperor. And yet we saved the Japanese culture. We let them keep their emperor; we let them keep their language; we let them keep their religion; we let them keep their customs. We took care of the defense for forty years. We built them up to be one of the strongest economies in the world.[201]

The more you give, Hudson says, the fuller your life, and World War II for him was giving. That night on Iwo Jima with his fellow Marines still comes back to him, the night Hudson heard life's hopes and dreams through the threat of death.

> I'll never forget that night because I just listened when each man spoke. I gave every man my ear and my heart, and while I listened to talk which ranged from love affairs to farms, I thought and took the best from each and formed my own ideas

on what I wanted in life and tried to make clear the picture of a hazy future that would be in store for me. I thought back to the first few days when I lost my closest friend, I thought of all the suffering that had gone on, that was going on at the time, and the suffering that will go on. I realized how lucky I was to be alive and that it really doesn't take much to be happy in life. I just wanted to live and re-member that night when I heard nine men tell of their doings, their hopes and wishes, their desires and aspirations, their fears and loves.

Glossary

Amtrac—Also called an LVT (for "landing vehicle, tracked"), the amtrac was a twenty-seven-foot long amphibious (operable on both land and water) vehicle with tracks. The first waves of Iwo Jima's invaders arrived in amtracs, which could carry about thirty-five infantrymen each.

BAR—Browning Automatic Rifle, called a "walking machine gun." A 30-06 caliber rapid-fire weapon that could be fired either from a bipod or standing up. An assistant carried ammunition and gear for each BAR man.

Bazooka—Over-the-shoulder rocket launcher used against fortified positions. One man, the gunner, held the tube while another loaded the shell from the back and tapped the gunner on the shoulder.

D-Day—The day appointed for starting an attack. The most famous D-Day was the June 6, 1944 landing on the beaches of Normandy.

DUKW—Amphibious vehicle eighteen feet long with four-wheel drive and rubber tires. One company of DUKWs (pronounced "ducks") was assigned to each Marine division at Iwo Jima.

Flamethrower—A portable weapon that shot jellied gasoline or another flammable fuel. Its five gallons of fuel lasted about seven seconds. Kuribayashi recommended to his superiors in his "lessons learned" for future combat, that if the Japanese wanted to hold a position, the flamethrower operators had to be neutralized.

H-Hour—The hour appointed for a starting an attack.

Hand grenade—A hand-held bomb that would go off a few seconds after pulling the pin (or in the case of a Japanese grenade, hitting it on a hard object).

Kabar—Solid, six-inch fixed blade knife issued to Marines, named for the major manufacturer.

Knee mortar—Japanese small-caliber mortar that could be fired and moved quickly by just one soldier.

LCI—Landing craft, infantry. The LCI, the LCT, the LCVP, and the LCM were called Higgins boats, flat-bottomed landing craft following a design by Andrew Higgins.

LCM—Landing craft, medium.

LCVP—Landing craft, vehicles, personnel. The craft had a hinged front that swung down for disembarking.

LCT—Landing craft, tank.

LST—Landing ship, tank. This large landing ship carried amtracs, DUKWs, and other heavy weapons and equipment.

Mortar—A short gun for firing shells at high angles. The sixty-millimeter mortar, which could reach eighteen hundred yards, needed a gunner, an assistant, and four carriers.

Satchel charge—Plastic explosive small enough to be carried by hand and thrown.

Shrapnel—Popular term for fragments from an explosive weapon.

Tracer—Bullet coated with phosphorus that burned in flight so the gunner could see where his bullets were going, especially at night.

Acknowledgements

I would like to thank Bill Hudson and his fellow Marines, along with World War II veterans in general, for the America in which I grew up. I would like to thank the original scientists of Los Alamos for my unique home town, where physicists were nothing special; they were just my friends' dads.

Thanks also to Bill Hudson for putting together his book *Once a Marine, Always a Marine* which provided a lot of the source material for this book. Anyone wishing to learn more about how the battle looked to a 19-year-old should read the rest of the letters he wrote home.

Thanks to the Pritzker Foundation for the use of their Hudson interview, which provided most of the rest of the source material for this book. Without that interview, I would have had to ask Bill Hudson to go through those memories yet again, and I don't have that level of chutzpah. Interested readers will find many intriguing details in the interview such as how to use cigars as mosquito repellent.

Thanks to Rosa Ogawa for permission to quote and fascinating background information on her father.

Thanks to the authors and publishers of the books and websites listed in my "Sources and Resources" from whom I learned so much more thought-provoking history than I could fit in this book. Special thanks to those who allowed me to use particularly striking quotations from the following:

www.atomicheritage.org by The Atomic Heritage Foundation

Atoms in the Family by Laura Fermi, published by University of Chicago Press

Downfall: The End of the Imperial Japanese Empire by Richard B. Frank, published by Penguin Books

Duty: A Father, His Son, and the Man Who Won the War by Bob Greene, published by HarperCollins

The 509th Remembered: A History of the 509th Composite Group as told by the Veterans that Dropped the Atomic Bombs on Japan, edited by Robert and Amelia Krauss, published by Robert Krauss

Grunts: Inside the American Infantry Combat Experience, World War II through Iraq by John McManus, published by Penguin Group

Iwo Jima: Amphibious Epic by Whitman Bartley, published by the United States Marine Corps History Division

Iwo Jima: World War II Veterans Remember the Greatest Battle of the Pacific by Larry Smith, published by W.W. Norton & Company

The Lions of Iwo Jima: The story of Combat Team 28 and the bloodiest battle in Marine Corps history by Major General Fred Haynes USMC (Ret.) and James A Warren, published by Henry Holt and Company.

Thanks to my family and extended family who encouraged, edited, financed, and asked hard questions about this effort.

Thanks to several friends who gave me feedback on the manuscript, especially my friend who encouraged me for twenty years to write something more interesting than a manual on properly signed-off plutonium transfers.

Karen Jo Tallentire, 2014

Sources and Resources

Atomic Archive. National Science Digital Library. http://www.atomicarchive.com.

Atomic Heritage Foundation. http://www.atomicheritage.org.

Barrella, Carron. More than 36 Days: Four Ordinary Men Face Extraordinary Circumstances. 2011. http://www.morethan36days.com

Bartley, Lt Col Whitman S. (USMC). *Iwo Jima: Amphibious Epic*. Washington DC: Historical Branch, U.S. Marine Corps, 1957.

Botkin Geoff. *League of Grateful Sons*. DVD. Faith of Our Fathers Project, Vision Forum Ministries, 2005.

Brady, James. *Why Marines Fight*. New York: Thomas Dunne Books, 2007.

Brode, Bernice. *Tales of Los Alamos: Life on the Mesa 1943-1945*. Los Alamos, NM: Los Alamos Historical Society, 1997.

Buell, Hal. Uncommon Valor, Common Virtue: Iwo Jima and the Photograph that Captured America. New York: The Berkley Publishing Group, 2006.

Chang, Iris. The Rape of Nanking: The Forgotten Holocaust of World War II. New York: Penguin Books, 1998.

Chapin, First Lieutenant John C. (USMCR). *The 4th Marine Division in World War II*. History and Museums Division, Headquarters, U.S. Marine Corps, Washington, D.C., 1974 reprint of 1945 edition.

Chicago Tribune. "Stamp Debate is Mushrooming." http://articles.chicagotribune.com/1995-03-01/features/9503010121_1_commemorative-stamps-postage-mushroom-cloud.

Department of Defense Stress Awareness. "Combat Stress." http://www.defense.gov/specials/stressawareness03/combat.html.

Department of the Navy. "US Navy and Marine Corps Personnel Casualties in World War II." http://www.history.navy.mil/faqs/faq11-1.htm#anchor2118718.

Dockery, Kevin. *Navy SEALs: A History of the Early Years*. New York: The Berkeley Publishing Group, 2001.

Fermi, Laura. *Atoms in the Family: My Life with Enrico Fermi*. Chicago: The University of Chicago Press, 1954.

Feynman, Richard P. *"Surely You're Joking, Mr. Feynman!" Adventures of a Curious Character*. Edited by Ralph Leighton and Edward Hutchings. New York: W.W. Norton & Company, Inc., 1985

5th Marine Division.com. http://www.5thmarinedivision.com/d31-to-d35.html.

509th Composite Group. "Manhattan Project." http://www.enolagay509th.com/manhat.htm.

Frank, Richard B. *Downfall: The End of the Imperial Japanese Empire*. New York: Penguin Books, 1999.

Gallagher, Thomas. *Assault in Norway: Sabotaging the Nazi Nuclear Bomb*. Guilford, Connecticut: The Lyons Press, 2002.

Glines, Carroll V. *The Doolittle Raid: America's daring first strike against Japan*. Atglen, Pennsylvania: Schiffer Publishing Ltd., 1991.

Goudsmit, Samuel A. *Alsos*. History of Modern Physics, 1800-1950; vol.1. Los Angeles/San Francisco: Tomash Publishers, 1983.

Greene, Bob. Duty: A Father, His Son, and the Man Who Won the War. New York: HarperCollins, 2000.

Haynes, Major General Fred (USMC-ret) and James A. Warren. *The Lions of Iwo Jima*. New York: Henry Holt and Company, 2008.

Held, E.B. *A Spy's Guide to Santa Fe and Albuquerque*. Albuquerque: University of New Mexico Press, 2011.

Henri, Raymond. *Iwo Jima: Springboard to Final Victory*. New York: U.S. Camera Publishing Corporation, 1945.

HonorYourVeteran.com. "Medal History & Protocol: The Medal of Honor." http://honoryourveteran.com/protocol/.

Hudson, William A. *Once A Marine, Always A Marine*. Unpublished Manuscript, Summer 1999. Photocopy.

Hudson, William A. *Oral History of William Hudson, World War II Marine*. Transcript of recorded interview by Paul Stillwell. USMC Collection, Pritzker Military Museum and Library, Chicago, 2005.

IwoJimaHistory.com. http://iwojimahistory.com/content/view/50/35/.

Jones, R.V. Introduction to *Alsos*, by Samuel A. Goudsmit. History of Modern Physics, 1800-1950; vol. 1.Los Angeles/San Francisco: Tomash Publishers, 1983.

Kim, Dong-Won. *Yoshio Nishina: Father of Modern Physics in Japan*. Boca Raton, Florida: Taylor & Francis Group, Inc., 2007.

Krauss, Robert and Amelia, eds. The 509th Remembered: A History of the 509th Composite Group as Told by the Veterans That Dropped the Atomic Bombs on Japan. Rev. ed. Buchanan, MI: 509th Press, 2009.

Leatherneck Marine Corps online community. http://www.leatherneck.com.

Los Alamos Historical Society. http://www.losalamoshistory.org.

Los Alamos National Laboratory Periodic Table of Elements. "Fermium." http://periodic.lanl.gov/100.shtml.

Los Alamos National Laboratory. "Our History." http://www.lanl.gov/history/people/nobel.shtml.

Los Angeles Times. "Japan Objects to Atomic Bomb Stamps." http://articles.latimes.com/1994-12-03/news/mn-4234_1_atomic-bomb.

Lyon, Fern, and Jacob Evans, eds. *Los Alamos: The First Forty Years*. Los Alamos, NM: Los Alamos Historical Society, 1984.

Maas, Dr. James B. Power Sleep: The Revolutionary Program That Prepares Your Mind for Peak Performance. New York: Quill, 1998.

Makos, Adam, and Marcus Brotherton. *Voices of the Pacific: Untold Stories from the Marine Heroes of World War II*. New York: The Berkeley Publishing Group, 2013.

Manhattan Project, The: an interactive history. https://www.osti.gov/manhattan-project-history.

Marine Corps Association & Foundation. Simpson, Ross W. "From Leatherneck: Iwo Jima: A Surgeon's Story." Originally published in Leatherneck Magazine February 1990. http://www.mca-marines.org/gazette/leatherneck-iwo-jima-surgeons-story.

The Marine Corps Medal of Honor Recipients. "Justice M. Chambers." http://www.marinemedals.com/chambersjustice.htm.

Marling, Karal and John Wetenhall. *Iwo Jima: Monuments, Memories, and the American Hero*. Harvard University Press, 1991.

McManus, John C. Grunts: Inside the American Infantry Combat Experience, World War II Through Iraq. New York: Penguin Group, 2010.

Morison, Samuel Eliot. *History of United States Naval Operations in World War II*, Volume XIV, Victory in the Pacific: 1945. ibiblio.org: http://www.ibiblio.org/hyperwar/USN/USN-Ops-XIV/USN-XIV-5.html.

The National Museum of the Marine Corps. "World War II Gallery." http://www.usmcmuseum.com/Exhibits_UncommonValor.asp.

National Park Service. "Home of Franklin D. Roosevelt National Historic Site." http://www.nps.gov/nr/travel/presidents/fdr_home.html.

Navy Department Library, The. "Justice M. Chambers, Lieutenant Colonel, USMCR." http://www.history.navy.mil/library/online/mohiwojima_chambers.htm.

Newcomb, Richard F. Abandon Ship! The Saga of the U.S.S. Indianapolis, the Navy's Greatest Sea Disaster. New York: Harper Collins, 2001.

Newcomb, Richard F. *Iwo Jima*. New York: Bantam Books, 1965.

Okabe, Tatsumi. *Revival of Japanese Militarism?* Singapore: Institute of Southeast Asian Studies, Occasional Paper No. 22, July 1974.

Prange, Gordon W., Donald M. Goldstein, and Katherine V. Dillon. *God's Samurai: Lead Pilot at Pearl Harbor*. Washington, D.C.: Prange Enterprises, Inc., 1990.

Proehl, Carl W., ed. *The Fourth Marine Division In World War II.* Washington: Infantry Journal Press, 1946.

Roensch, Eleanor Stone. *Life Within Limits.* Los Alamos, NM: Los Alamos Historical Society, 1993.

Running 50. "Medal of Honor Recipient Staff Sgt. Ty Carter on Morning Joe." http://running50.com/medal-of-honor-recipient-staff-sgt-ty-carter-on-morning-joe/.

Russell, Michael. *Iwo Jima.* New York: Ballantine Books, 1974.

Saluting American Valor. "The Medals." http://www.americanvalor.net/medals.

Segre, Emilio. *Enrico Fermi: Physicist.* Chicago and London: University of Chicago Press, 1970.

Shirer, William L. The Rise and Fall of the Third Reich: A History of Nazi Germany. New York: Fawcett Crest, 1960.

Smith, Larry. Iwo Jima: World War II Veterans Remember the Greatest Battle of the Pacific. New York: W.W. Norton & Company, 2008.

Stamp News Now. "The Banned A-Bomb Stamp." http://www.stampnewsnow.com/PDF_Pages/a-bombSamplePage.pdf.

Stars and Stripes. Schogol, Jeff. "Are Purple Hearts from 1945 still being awarded?" September 1, 2010. http://www.stripes.com/blogs/the-rumor-doctor/the-rumor-doctor-1.104348/are-purple-hearts-from-1945-still-being-awarded-1.116756.

Sulzberger, C.L. *World War II.* New York: McGraw-Hill Book Company, 1970.

Sun Tzu. *The Art of War.* Translated by Lionel Giles. The Internet Classics Archive, Daniel C. Stephenson, 2009. http://classics.mit.edu/Tzu/artwar.html.

Szasz, Ferenc Morton. The Day the Sun Rose Twice: The Story of the Trinity Site Nuclear Explosion July 16, 1945. Albuquerque: University of New Mexico Press, 1984.

Tibbets, Paul W. Jr. with Clair C. Stebbins and Harry Franken. *The Tibbets Story.* New York: Stein and Day, 1978.

Theismann, Jeanne. "Survivors Reunite for 68th Anniversary of Iwo Jima." *Black Sands,* summer 2013. http://www.iwojimaassociation.org/images/newsletter/blacksands-vol-04-issue-01-2013-summer.pdf.

The United States Army Air Forces in World War II.
http://www.usaaf.net/ww2/airlift.

Truman, Harry S. *Memoirs by Harry S. Truman*. Volume One: Year of
Decisions. Garden City, NY: Doubleday & Company, Inc., 1955.

Unit 731. http://www.unit731.org.

University of New Mexico Bureau of Business and Economic
Research. "Presentation on Los Alamos County." January 2003.
https://bber.unm.edu/publs/losalamosco.pdf.

University of North Carolina Wilmington Abrons Student Health
Center. "Instruction Sheet: Foreign Body Left in Wound."
http://uncw.edu/healthservices/documents/DCSheet-
ForeighBodyLeftinWound09.pdf.

USMC Training and Education Command (TECOM) website, US
Marine Corps. Accessed May 24, 2012,
http://www.tecom.usmc.mil.

US Department of Defense. "Military Awards for Valor – Top 3."
http://valor.defense.gov/DescriptionofAwards.aspx.

US Postal Service. "Publicity Kit: Medal of Honor: World War II
Forever Stamps." http://about.usps.com/postal-
bulletin/2013/pb22375/html/cover.htm.

USS Indianapolis website. "Captain McVay."
http://www.ussindianapolis.org.

"'Utter Destruction,' Promised in Potsdam Ultimatum, Unleashed;
Power Equals 2,000 Superforts." *Santa Fe New Mexican*. Monday,
August 6, 1945.

Voices of the Manhattan Project. http://manhattanprojectvoices.org.

Wachi, Tsunezo. "The August Virtue of His Imperial Majesty."
Translated by Rosa Ogawa. January 1989.
http://www.marineswwii.com/pdfs/August%20Virtue.pdf.

Wikipedia. http://en.wikipedia.org/wiki.

Wilson, Jane S., and Charlotte Serber, eds. *Standing By and Making
Do: Women of Wartime Los Alamos*. Los Alamos, NM: Los
Alamos Historical Society, 1997.

Warren, James A. American Spartans: The U.S. Marines: A Combat
History from Iwo Jima to Iraq. New York: Free Press, 2005.

World War II Database. http://ww2db.com.

WWII Wiki. "Banzai Charge." http://world-war-
2.wikia.com/wiki/Banzai_Charge.

Endnotes

[1] William A. Hudson, transcript of recorded interview by Paul Stillwell, *Oral History of William Hudson, World War II Marine*, (Chicago: USMC Collection, Pritzker Military Museum and Library, 2005), 34.

[2] This quote and all other quotes without other references are from William A. Hudson, *Once A Marine, Always A Marine*, (Unpublished Manuscript, Summer 1999).

[3] Hudson, *Oral History*, 36.

[4] John C. McManus, Grunts: Inside the American Infantry Combat Experience, World War II Through Iraq, (New York: Penguin Group, 2010), 67.

[5] Haynes and Warren, *Lions of Iwo Jima*, 91.

[6] Only 99 of 30,000, according to Haynes and Warren, *Lions of Iwo Jima*, 90.

[7] Hudson, *Oral History*, 37.

[8] Hudson, *Oral History*, 36.

[9] Hudson, *Oral History*, 59.

[10] Hudson, *Oral History*, 59.

[11] Hudson, *Oral History*, 37.

[12] Hudson, *Oral History*, 37.

[13] Hudson, *Oral History*, 35.

[14] Hudson, *Oral History*, 1.

[15] Hudson, *Oral History*, 3.

[16] Hudson, *Oral History*, 3.

[17] Hudson, *Oral History*, 5.

[18] Hudson, *Oral History*, 15.

[19] Hudson, *Oral History*, 15.

[20] Hudson, *Oral History*, 3.

[21] Hudson, *Oral History*, 6.

[22] Hudson, *Oral History*, 6.

[23] Hudson, *Oral History*, 6.

[24] Hudson, *Oral History*, 6.

[25] Hudson, *Oral History*, 6.

[26] Hudson, *Oral History*, 6.

[27] Larry Smith, *Iwo Jima: World War II Veterans Remember the Greatest Battle of the Pacific* (New York: W.W. Norton & Company, 2008), 28. Quoting Corporal James "Salty" Hathaway Amtrac Crew Chief, Tenth Amtrac Battalion, Fourth Marine Division.

[28] Hudson, *Oral History*, 9.

[29] Hudson, *Oral History*, 9.

[30] Hudson, *Oral History*, 12.

[31] Hudson, *Oral History*, 12.

[32] Hudson, *Oral History*, 12.

[33] Hudson, *Oral History*, 13.

[34] Hudson, *Oral History*, 17.

[35] Lt Col Whitman S. Bartley, (USMC), *Iwo Jima: Amphibious Epic* (Washington DC: Historical Branch, U.S. Marine Corps, 1957), 44.

[36] Hudson, *Oral History*, 19.

[37] Hudson, *Oral History*, 19-20.

[38] Smith, *Iwo Jima*, 223. Quoting Pharmacist's Mate Third Class George Wahlen, Navy Corpsman; Medal of Honor, Twenty-sixth Marines, Fifth Marine Division.

[39] Hudson, *Oral History*, 22.

[40] Hudson, *Oral History*, 46.

[41] Sun Tzu, *The Art of War*, trans. Lionel Giles (The Internet Classics Archive, Daniel C. Stephenson: 2009), XI, 4, http://classics.mit.edu/Tzu/artwar.html.

[42] Tsunezo Wachi, "The August Virtue of His Imperial Majesty," trans. Rosa Ogawa (January 1989), http://www.marineswwii.com/pdfs/August%20Virtue.pdf.

[43] Hudson, *Oral History*, 34.

[44] Hudson, *Oral History*, 35.

[45] Hudson, *Oral History*, 34.

[46] Bob Greene, *Duty: A Father, His Son, and the Man Who Won the War*, (New York: HarperCollins, 2000), 164. Quoting Paul Tibbets, pilot of the *Enola Gay*.

[47] Hudson, *Oral History*, 38.

[48] Hudson, *Oral History*, 57.

[49] Hudson, *Oral History*, 38.

[50] Based on 110,000 Marines and supporting forces, plus 22,000 Japanese over 8.5 square miles of island. Haynes and Warren, *Lions of Iwo Jima*, 4-8.

[51] Hudson, *Oral History*, 55.

[52] Hudson, *Oral History*, 30.

[53] Hudson, *Oral History*, 38.

[54] Bartley, Iwo Jima: Amphibious Epic, 142.

[55] Smith, *Iwo Jima*, 83. Quoting Corporal Glenn Buzzard, Machine Gunner, Twenty-fourth Marines, Fourth Marine Division, Two Purple Hearts.

[56] Hudson, *Oral History*, 63.

[57] Hudson, *Oral History*, 29.

[58] Hudson, *Oral History*, 40.

[59] Hudson, *Oral History*, 39.

[60] William A. Hudson, *Once A Marine, Always A Marine,* (Unpublished Manuscript, Summer 1999), "Iwo Jima".

[61] Hudson, *Oral History*, 32.

[62] Hudson, *Oral History*, 43.

[63] Hudson, *Oral History*, 43.

[64] Hudson, *Oral History*, 43.

[65] Hudson, *Oral History*, 65.

[66] "Justice M. Chambers, Lieutenant Colonel, USMCR," The Navy Department Library, http://www.history.navy.mil/library/online/mohiwojima_chambers.htm

[67] Hudson, *Oral History*, 29-30.

[68] Hudson, *Oral History*, 29.

[69] Hudson, *Oral History*, 30.

[70] Hudson, *Oral History*, 40.

[71] Hudson, *Oral History*, 86.

[72] Hudson, *Oral History*, 45.

[73] Personal experiences of combat fatigue are told in Adam Makos and Marcus Brotherton, *Voices of the Pacific: Untold Stories from the Marine Heroes of World War II* (The Berkeley Publishing Group, New York, 2013), 278-279, 281-282, 324-325, 340.

[74] Hudson, *Oral History*, 87.

[75] Hudson, *Oral History*, 87.

[76] Hudson, *Oral History*, 2.

[77] Sun Tzu, *Art of War*, II, 7.

[78] Hudson, *Oral History*, 42.

[79] Hudson, *Oral History*, 42.

[80] Hudson, *Oral History*, 42.

[81] Hudson, *Oral History*, 55.

[82] Hudson, *Oral History*, 55.

[83] Hudson, *Oral History*, 56.

[84] Haynes and Warren, *Lions of Iwo Jima*, 176. Quoting Sgt. Francis W. Cockrel, combat correspondent with Combat Team 28.

[85] There were 2880 casualties in the Fourth Division from the Meat Grinder according to Richard F. Newcomb, *Iwo Jima* (New York: Bantam Books, 1965), 187.

[86] Hudson, *Oral History*, 61.

[87] Hudson, *Oral History*, 61.

[88] Hudson, *Oral History*, 63.

[89] Hudson, *Oral History*, 63.

[90] Hudson, *Oral History*, 56.

[91] Hudson, *Oral History*, 56.

[92] Hudson, *Oral History*, 49.

[93] Hudson, *Oral History*, 49.

[94] Hudson, *Oral History*, 49.

[95] Hudson, *Oral History*, 61.

[96] Hudson, *Oral History*, 61.

[97] Hudson, *Oral History*, 47.

[98] Hudson, *Oral History*, 46.

[99] According to Col John W. Ripley, USMC (Ret), former director of history and museums for the Marine Corps, replacements were lost on a scale of two to one compared to veterans. Smith, *Iwo Jima*, 331.

[100] Hudson, *Oral History*, 48.

[101] Hudson, *Oral History*, 28.

[102] Hudson, *Oral History*, 48.

[103] Hudson, *Oral History*, 48.

[104] Haynes and Warren, *Lions of Iwo Jima*, 198. Quoting MGen Fred Haynes, captain at Iwo Jima.

[105] Hudson, *Oral History*, 64.

[106] Hudson, *Oral History*, 62.

[107] Hudson, *Oral History*, 62.

[108] Hudson, *Oral History*, 45.

[109] Hudson, *Once a Marine, Always a Marine*, Letter from Manuel Martinez to Bill Hudson, July 20, 1999.

[110] Hudson, *Oral History*, 50.

[111] Hudson, *Oral History*, 50.

[112] Hudson, *Oral History*, 50-51.

[113] Hudson, *Oral History*, 51.

[114] Hudson, *Oral History*, 51.

[115] Hudson, *Oral History*, 51.

[116] Hudson, *Oral History*, 51-52.

[117] Hudson, *Oral History*, 52.

[118] Hudson, *Oral History*, 52.

[119] From Nimitz's Pacific Fleet Communique No. 300 of 17 March 1945.

[120] The main fighting was 19 February to 26 March. Haynes and Warren, *Lions of Iwo Jima*, 6.

[121] Total casualties who lived include 19,217 wounded, of whom 17,272 were Marines, and 2,648 combat fatigue victims, of whom all were Marines. Hal Buell, *Uncommon Valor, Common Virtue: Iwo Jima and the Photograph that Captured America*. (The Berkley Publishing Group, New York, 2006), 219.

[122] Maybe 92%, maybe more. For details, see following notes about battle statistics.

[123] Based on 110,000 Marines and supporting forces, plus 22,000 Japanese over 8.5 square miles of island. Haynes and Warren, *Lions of Iwo Jima*, 4-8.

[124] Based on about 20,000 Japanese plus about 7000 Americans, divided by 8.5 square miles, from Haynes and Warren, *Lions of Iwo Jima*, 4, 8. Newcomb, *Iwo Jima*, 243, quotes Seabee Captain Johnson as saying 550 Americans died and 2500 were wounded for every square mile.

[125] Based on about 20,000 Japanese plus about 7000 Americans. Haynes and Warren, *Lions of Iwo Jima*, 8 lists 22,000 defenders, 28,000 American casualties, fewer than 2000 surviving Japanese.

[126] Haynes and Warren, *Lions of Iwo Jima*, 60.

[127] Based on 216 prisoners divided by 22,000 total Japanese. Haynes and Warren, *Lions of Iwo Jima*, 8, 77.

[128] That is, at least 1,600 of 22,000, based on over 1600 Japanese who later surrendered. Smith, *Iwo Jima*, xxi.

[129] Based on 22,000 Japanese on the island (Haynes and Warren, *Lions of Iwo Jima*, 8), 216 prisoners, and 1600 who surrendered after the battle, from Smith, *Iwo Jima*, xxi. According to James A. Warren, *American Spartans: The U.S. Marines: A Combat History from Iwo Jima to Iraq* (New York: Free Press, 2005), 35, the figure would be 99%, but he appears not to be counting those who later surrendered. In Smith, *Iwo Jima*, 321, Colonel John W. Ripley points out that at least a couple thousand of "Japanese" losses were Korean laborers.

[130] Haynes and Warren, *Lions of Iwo Jima*, 31.

[131] Haynes and Warren, *Lions of Iwo Jima*, 4.

[132] Smith, *Iwo Jima*, 336. Quoting Colonel John W. Ripley, USMC (Ret.) former director of history and museums for the Marine Corps.

[133] Based on 75,000 Marines, 25,000 casualties, 7,000 killed, as stated in Smith, *Iwo Jima*, 329-330. Quoting Col John W. Ripley, USMC (Ret), former director of history and museums for the Marine Corps.

[134] Hudson, *Oral History*, 46.

[135] Of these aircraft, 280 actually bombed Tokyo according to Smith, *Iwo Jima*, 276-277.

[136] Sun Tzu, *The Art of War*, XII, 3-4.

[137] Subtracting 1903 from 1945 means any officers over about 42 years old were born before Kitty Hawk.

[138] Sun Tzu, *The Art of War*, XI, 57.

[139] Hudson, *Oral History*, 62.

[140] Numbers vary, according to Warren, *American Spartans*, 92.

[141] Wachi, "August Virtue."

[142] A very detailed analysis of Japan's terrible military and economic situation by 1945, and their attitude about defending their homeland anyway, is in Richard B. Frank, *Downfall: The End of the Imperial Japanese Empire*, (New York: Penguin Books, 1999), particularly pages 189-190.

[143] 7613 dead over 51 days, according to "Okinawa Campaign," World War II Database, http://ww2db.com/battle_spec.php?battle_id=15.

[144] Hudson, *Oral History*, 27.

[145] Hudson, *Oral History*, 27.

[146] Hudson, *Oral History*, 27.

[147] Hudson, *Oral History*, 27.

[148] Hudson, *Oral History*, 27.

[149] Hudson, *Oral History*, 46.

[150] Frank, *Downfall*, 127.

[151] Hudson, *Oral History*, 69.

[152] Hudson, *Oral History*, 69.

[153] Hudson, *Oral History*, 70.

[154] Hudson, *Oral History*, 70.

[155] Hudson, *Oral History*, 70.

[156] Hudson, *Oral History*, 13.

[157] Hudson, *Oral History*, 13.

[158] Hudson, *Oral History*, 71.

[159] Hudson, *Oral History*, 71.

[160] Greene, *Duty*, 168.

[161] Hudson, *Oral History*, 72.

[162] Hudson, *Oral History*, 72.

[163] Hudson, *Oral History*, 71.

[164] Krauss, Robert and Amelia, eds., The 509th Remembered: A History of the 509th Composite Group as Told by the Veterans That Dropped the Atomic Bombs on Japan, rev. ed. (Buchanan, MI: 509th Press, 2009), 112.

[165] Col Paul Tibbets, speech from his first meeting with the 509th. Quoted in Krauss, *The 509th Remembered*, 214.

[166] Sun Tzu, *Art of War*, III, 1-2.

[167] For instance, 45,000 in Hamburg and 60,000 in Dresden from Allied bombing, 90,000-100,000 in Tokyo from the firebombing, and 250,000-350,000 in the Rape of Nanking. Frank, *Downfall*, 41, 46, 334-337; Chang, *Rape of Nanking*, 6.

[168] "By most accounts the number of dead was half that of Hiroshima," Frank, *Downfall*, 285.

[169] Dr. Hachiya, quoted in Frank, *Downfall*, 321.

[170] Smith, *Iwo Jima*, 40. Quoting Corporal James "Salty" Hathaway Amtrac Crew Chief, Tenth Amtrac Battalion, Fourth Marine Division.

[171] Smith, *Iwo Jima*, 71. Quoting Corporal Hershel Woodrow "Woody" Williams, Medal of Honor, Twenty-first Marines, Third Marine Division.

[172] Smith, *Iwo Jima*, 272. Quoting Staff Sergeant Valentine Chepeleff, Radar Bombardier, B-29, Fortieth Squadron, Sixth Bomb Group.

[173] Smith, *Iwo Jima*, 291. Quoting Lieutenant Phil True, B-29 Navigator, Ninety-ninth Squadron, Ninth Bomb Group.

[174] Greene, *Duty*, 258.

[175] Haynes and Warren, *Lions of Iwo Jima*, 158-159.

[176] Greene, *Duty*, 288.

[177] Krauss, The 509th Remembered, 131.

[178] Hudson, *Oral History*, 70.

[179] Wachi, "August Virtue"

[180] Wachi, "August Virtue"

[181] Hudson, *Oral History*, 73.

[182] Hudson, *Oral History*, 70.

[183] Hudson, *Oral History*, 70.

[184] Hudson, *Oral History*, 70.

[185] Hudson, *Oral History*, 70.

[186] Hudson, *Oral History*, 75.

[187] Hudson, *Oral History*, 75.

[188] Hudson, *Oral History*, 75.

[189] "The Einstein Letter - 1939," Atomic Heritage Foundation, http://www.atomicheritage.org/history/einstein-letter-1939.

[190] Jane S. Wilson and Charlotte Serber, eds., *Standing By and Making Do: Women of Wartime Los Alamos*, (Los Alamos, NM: Los Alamos Historical Society, 1997), 25, 46.

[191] Laura Fermi, *Atoms in the Family: My Life with Enrico Fermi* (Chicago: 1954 by The University of Chicago), 226.

[192] Fermi, *Atoms*, 232.

[193] Hudson, *Oral History*, 66.

[194] Hudson, *Oral History*, 46.

[195] Greene, *Duty*, 186.

[196] Hudson, *Oral History*, 30.

[197] Hudson, *Oral History*, 30.

[198] Hudson, *Oral History*, 79.

[199] Hudson, *Oral History*, 57.

[200]No one really knows how many Iwo Jima veterans are still alive, but it is obvious they are quickly becoming fewer. Jeanne Theismann, "Survivors Reunite for 68th Anniversary of Iwo Jima," *Black Sands*, Summer 2013, http://www.iwojimaassociation.org/images/newsletter/blacksands-vol-04-issue-01-2013-summer.pdf.

[201] Hudson, *Oral History*, 76.

CPSIA information can be obtained
at www.ICGtesting.com
Printed in the USA
FSOW02n0721260115
4773FS